POLITICAL SHORTS

1,001 OF THE FUNNIEST POLITICAL ONE-LINERS

GLENN LIEBMAN

CB
CONTEMPORARY BOOKS

Library of Congress Cataloging-in-Publication Data

Political shorts : 1,001 of the funniest one-liners / [compiled by]
  Glenn Liebmann.
     p.   cm.
  ISBN 0-8092-2780-0
    1. Political science—Quotations, maxims, etc.   2. Politicians—
Quotations—Humor.   I. Liebmann, Glenn.
PN6084.P6P64   1999
320'.2'07—dc21   98-54960
                                                  CIP

Jacket illustration copyright © Mark Anderson
Jacket design by Todd Petersen

Published by Contemporary Books
A division of NTC/Contemporary Publishing Group, Inc.
4255 West Touhy Avenue, Lincolnwood (Chicago), Illinois 60646-1975 U.S.A.
Copyright © 1999 by Glenn Liebman

Printed in the United States of America
International Standard Book Number: 0-8092-2780-0

99 00 01 02 03 04 LB 18 17 16 15 14 13 12 11 10 9 8 7 6 5 4 3 2 1

To Kathy:
Thank you for your love,
support, enthusiasm, and inspiration.

ACKNOWLEDGMENTS

This book would not have been possible without the help of my agent, Philip Spitzer, and my editors at NTC/Contemporary, John Nolan and Craig Bolt. All three have been a pleasure to work with on this project.

I'd also like to thank some of my friends who are as interested in politics as I am. David Agler and I have had many a political discussion over the last twenty-five years (it's cold in Oswego). I can't remember a time when Scott Sommer and I were not discussing politics. He was working his first campaign when he was still in his mother's womb.

Thanks to my friends David and Sue Wollner and their wonderful sons Michael, Sam, and Andrew. David and I have spent much of our adult lives discussing politics when we are not obsessing about mutual funds.

Thanks also to Rita Stein, Tom Precious, and their great kids, Ariel and Zachy. One of the highlights of the last few years has been our friendship with them.

When I am not working on quotation books, I am the executive director of the Alliance for the Mentally Ill of New York State. In this capacity I have had the honor of working alongside five board presidents: Joe Gentile, Ken Goldstein, Jerry Klein, Roy Neville, and Ike Rubin. All have served the organization with honor and intelligence. They have been tremendous to work with and have taught me a lot about life. I have great admiration for all of them.

I also have great admiration for three of the most important people in New York's mental-health system--New York Assembly Mental Health Chair, James Brennan; New York Senate Mental Health Chair, Thomas Libous; and New York's Mental Health Commissioner, James Stone. They have been able to put aside partisan politics to create a more optimistic future for people with mental illness and their families.

I'd also like to thank my family for their support and encouragement. My mother-in-law, Helen Coll, is a wonderful person—she defies every stereotype of mothers-in-law. My father, Bernie, continues to teach me lessons about persistence and believing in myself. My mother, Frieda, taught me about compassion and friendship. If she were alive, *Political Shorts* would be a bestseller because she would max out on fifty credit cards to buy every copy she could get her hands on.

My brother, Bennett, continues to be a major inspiration in my life. His decency and intelligence are evident to anyone who meets him. He also probably knows more trivia about New York politics than anyone.

I'd like to thank my son, Frankie, who gives me more pleasure than I ever thought possible. Every day with him is a delight. In the last four years, he has taught me more about enthusiasm for life than I learned in my first thirty-six years. In addition, he has the largest collection of sticks in all of upstate New York.

Finally, the person most responsible for the good things in life has been my wife, Kathy. She will always be my closest friend and confidant. I am lucky she is the focal point of my life.

INTRODUCTION

It is amazing how seemingly insignificant things can greatly affect one's life. When I turned fifteen, I became too old for the day camp I had attended the previous five years; and I was too young to get working papers. (Of course, I still could have worked anyway.) So at age fifteen, I had a free summer. It was the summer I fell in love.

I fell in love not with a woman but with Sam Ervin, Sam Dash, Howard Baker, and everyone else involved in the Watergate hearings. It was gripping television.

I am convinced that my course of life changed after those hearings. For most of the last twenty-five years, I have been involved in politics. My graduate degree was in political science. I worked in the administration of New York's former governor Mario Cuomo. And now I am the lobbyist for the Alliance for the Mentally Ill of New York State.

Had my parents been harder on me twenty-five

years ago and forced me to work, I am sure that my ultimate career path would have been completely different.

My fascination with politics had resulted in an extensive collection of one-liners from the best and brightest—as well as some who are not the best and not very bright—of the world of politics. Putting this book together has been a labor of love.

Whether you're a rabid Republican ("Republicans believe every day is the Fourth of July, but Democrats believe every day is April 15" —Ronald Reagan) or a determined Democrat ("The Democratic Party at its worst is better for the country than the Republican party at its best" —Lyndon Johnson), the one thing that everyone can agree on is that humor is clearly a bipartisan issue.

ACT YOUR AGE

"It's the gray-haired ladies who come and say, 'Gee, you look exactly like my mother' that worries me a bit."

Barbara Bush, on the aging process

"By the time you reach my age, you've made plenty of mistakes if you've lived your life properly."
Ronald Reagan

"There are three periods in life—youth, middle age, and 'how well you look.'"
Nelson Rockefeller

SPIRO AGNEW

"You never had to ask his score. Just count the casualties."

Bob Hope, on Agnew's atrocious golf game

"When Agnew yelled 'fore,' you never knew whether he was telling someone to get out of the way or if he was predicting how many spectators he would hit with a shot."

Bob Hope

"I didn't vote for you, but you have a nice suit on."

Don Meredith, upon meeting Agnew during a Monday Night Football broadcast

"We're going to send Spiro in there with a golf club and a tennis racket."

Richard Nixon, on negotiations with Cambodia (Agnew recently had hit bystanders while playing golf and tennis)

ALL POLITICS IS LOCAL

"The kind of thing I'm good at is knowing every politician in the state and remembering where he itches. And I know where to scratch him."

Earl Long, on his days in Louisiana

AMBASSADOR

"I prefer to pay for my own vacations."
> *Walter Mondale, on why he would*
> *turn down ambassadorships to Great*
> *Britain and France*

"It was 95 percent ego and 5 percent patriotism. I think."
> *Robert Strauss, on accepting the*
> *position of ambassador to Moscow*
> *under the Bush administration*

ANIMAL KINGDOM

"It's true that I am a low, mean snake. But you, sir, could walk beneath me wearing a top hat."
> *Benjamin Disraeli, to an opponent*

"I'm afraid I can't use a mule. I have several hundred up on Capitol Hill."
> *Ronald Reagan, refusing a gift of a*
> *mule*

"I'm afraid the country is not ready for a president who might have a tiger tattooed on his rear end."

> *George Shultz, former secretary of state, on his possibly running for president*

APPOINTMENTS

"A few more fat old men wouldn't hurt the place."

> *Marlin Fitzwater, on President Clinton's early appointees*

"Every time I make one appointment, I make nine disappointments."

> *Bibb Graves, former Alabama governor*

"The mistake a lot of politicians make is in forgetting they've been appointed and thinking they've been anointed."

> *Claude Pepper*

CLEMENT ATTLEE

"He is a modest little man with much to be modest about."

> *Winston Churchill, on the former*
> *British prime minister*

"An empty taxi arrived at 10 Downing Street, and when the door was opened Attlee walked out."
> *Winston Churchill*

BASEBALL

"If you told him to bunt, he bunted."

> *Ethan Allen, on George Bush, whom*
> *he coached at Yale*

"He sat where I usually sit. I didn't have the heart to say move out."

> *Joe Altobelli, former Orioles manager,*
> *on President Reagan sitting in the*
> *Orioles' dugout*

"It was like Bush coming back to the Clinton inauguration."

> *Barry Bonds, on going back to play the Pirates after signing as a free agent with the Giants*

"He tried to burn it in there. I decided the main thing was to get it to the catcher."

> *Bill Clinton, on lobbing the ball to the plate on Opening Day the year after George Bush's attempt fell short of the catcher's mitt*

"Being a Cubs fan prepares you for life in Washington."

> *Hillary Clinton*

"I wouldn't rule out center field for the Yankees, either."

> *Mario Cuomo, asked if he was ruling out a presidential run*

"Hotter'n hell, ain't it, Prez?"

> *Babe Ruth, said to President Coolidge*

"Line them up and let them shoot jump shots from the key."

> *Bill Bradley, former NBA star, on how the Democrats should choose their presidential candidate*

"If I ever go to Russia to meet with Gorbachev, the news stories will start out, 'Bill Bradley, former New York Knick.'"

> *Bill Bradley, during his days as a senator from New Jersey*

"I think I've lost reelection in 1996 already, but we've been waiting so long for this game, it's worth it."

> *Bill Clinton, on showing his partisanship by rooting for the Arkansas Razorbacks in the NCAA championship game*

"It was the first time in my life I was happy to see zero after my name."

> *Tom McMillen, former NBA player and congressman, on having no bounced checks in the congressional check-writing scandal*

"You mean there aren't enough people mad at me already?"

> *Ronald Reagan, upon being presented with a referee's uniform during a visit from the NBA commissioner*

BED

"I hope the sheets have been changed."

> *Yitzhak Shamir, former Israeli prime minister, when told he had slept in the same bed in Bulgaria as Muammar Gadhafi*

"Politics makes strange bedfellows."
> *Charles Dudley Warner*

BEVERAGE OF CHOICE

"But that won't give me a free hand to hold the beer."

> *Billy Carter, while being taught a*
> *two-handed backhand by Chris Evert*

"The three-martini lunch is the epitome of American efficiency. Where else can you get an earful, a bellyful, and a snootful at the same time?"

> *Gerald Ford*

BOOK BEAT

"I'm trying to figure out what to do with them. No reasonable offer refused."

> *Jim Baen, publisher of Newt*
> *Gingrich's novel, on what he would*
> *do with the thousands of unsold*
> *copies*

"I write on airplanes. It's my version of golf, a way of breaking out, thinking differently."
Newt Gingrich

"Talking is more tiring than I thought."
Newt Gingrich, when asked how he was faring on a book tour

"I am being frank about myself in this book. I tell of my first mistake on page 850."
Henry Kissinger, on his second autobiography

"Politics is not a bad profession. If you succeed there are many rewards; if you disgrace yourself, you can always write a book."
Ronald Reagan

BOXING

"At least as honest as our political system."
Tex Cobb, on boxing's bizarre rating system

"I told the voters that after I finished speaking, we would show fight pictures. They had to stay and listen to me to see the movies. They stayed."

> *John Tunney, son of boxer Gene Tunney, on running for Congress and getting crowds for his speeches by promising to show tapes of his father's famous fights with Jack Dempsey*

BROTHERLY LOVE

"The White House doesn't try to restrict me—I don't think they even claim to know me anymore."

> *Billy Carter*

"Jimmy's still mad because I wouldn't take the secretary of state. I want to be director of alcohol and firearms."

> *Billy Carter*

"My brother Bob doesn't want to be in government—he promised Dad he'd go straight."

> *Barry Goldwater, contrasting his brother with Bobby Kennedy, who became attorney general*

"I can't see that it's wrong to give him a little legal experience before he goes out to practice law."

John F. Kennedy, on appointing his brother Bobby as attorney general

PATRICK BUCHANAN

"The idea that Patrick Buchanan wants to engage me on economic issues is laughable. I never duel with unarmed men."

Phil Gramm

WILLIAM F. BUCKLEY

"I'm intelligent enough to read William F. Buckley's column, but I'm not intellectual enough to finish it."

Marv Levy, former Buffalo Bills coach, on his history degree from Harvard

"Bureaucracy is a giant mechanism operated by pygmies."

Honoré de Balzac

"The nearest approach to immortality on earth is a government bureau."

James Byrnes, former congressman

"I'm surprised that a government organization could do it that quickly."

Jimmy Carter, on being told it took 20 years to build the Pyramids

"Bureaucracy is the death of any achievement."

Albert Einstein

"Federal regulations represent a threat to the imaginative capacities of the American people second only to daytime television."

A. Bartlett Giamatti, former commissioner of major-league baseball

"The moment you turn your back, the government has created another agency."

> *Lord Halifax, misunderstanding when golfer Gene Sarazen told him he was going to play in the PGA*

"Every revolution evaporates and leaves behind only the slime of a new bureaucracy."

> *Franz Kafka*

"Government is a swamp into which whole armies get lost."

> *Ed Koch*

"The only thing that saves us from the bureaucracy is its inefficiency."

> *Eugene McCarthy*

"The single most exciting thing you encounter in government is competence, because it's so rare."

> *Daniel Patrick Moynihan*

"If we did not have such a thing as airplanes today, we would probably create something the size of NASA to make one."

> *H. Ross Perot*

"Anything that the private sector can do, government can do worse."

> *Dixie Lee Ray, former governor of Washington*

"Government does not solve problems—it subsidizes them."

> *Ronald Reagan*

"The nine most terrifying words in the English language are 'I'm from the government and I'm here to help.' "

> *Ronald Reagan*

"Government is like a big baby—an alimentary canal with a big appetite at one end and no sense of responsibility at the other."

> *Ronald Reagan*

"There's enough fat in the government in Washington that if it was . . . made into soap, it would wash the world."

> *Ronald Reagan*

"Dealing with the State Department is like watching an elephant become pregnant."
Franklin Roosevelt

BUREAUCRATS

"The perfect bureaucrat . . . is the man who manages to make no decisions and escape all responsibilities."
Brooks Atkinson

"A bureaucrat is a Democrat who holds some office that a Republican wants."
Alben Barkley

"Some civil servants are neither servants nor civil."
Winston Churchill

"If there's anything a public servant hates to do, it's something for the public."
Kin Hubbard

"Everybody in government is like a bunch of ants on a log floating down a river. Each one thinks he is guarding the log, but it's really just going with the flow."

Robert Strauss

GEORGE BUSH

"I married the first man I ever kissed. When I tell that to my children, they just about throw up."

Barbara Bush, on George

"Anyone who eats pork rinds can't be all good."

Barbara Bush, on her husband

"He'd rather face Congress than a three-foot putt."

Ken Raynor, golf pro at the
Kennebunk course where Bush plays

"He can't help it. He was born with a silver foot in his mouth."

Ann Richards, on all the
misstatements of President Bush

"I didn't vote for you, I didn't even think of voting for you, and I probably won't next time."

> *Robert Strauss, after being asked by*
> *President Bush to be ambassador to*
> *Moscow*

GEORGE W. BUSH

"If he can't run for office any better than he runs the Texas Rangers, he doesn't have an advantage."

> *Ed Martin, Texas Democratic party*
> *director, on George W. Bush running*
> *for governor of Texas and owning*
> *part of the Texas Rangers*

BUSINESS

"The best minds are not in government. If any were, business would hire them away."

> *Ronald Reagan*

CABINET

"We get along so well that when Cap and I are in Washington we have breakfast every week alone—except for our tasters."

> *Alexander Haig, Reagan's secretary of state, on his tumultuous relationship with Treasury Secretary Caspar Weinberger*

"I'd feel a helluva lot better if just one of them had ever run for sheriff."

> *Sam Rayburn, on the intellectuals in the cabinet and staff of President Kennedy*

CAMPAIGN TRAIL

"As a politician who loves to kiss babies, I'm looking forward to it."

> *Terry Branstad, Iowa governor, on the impending birth of septuplets in Iowa*

"I could not lose unless I was caught in bed with a dead girl or a live boy."

Edwin Edwards, on running for governor of Louisiana

"The biggest danger for a politician is to shake hands with a man who's physically stronger, has been drinking, and is voting for the other guy."

William Proxmire

"No matter how thin you slice it, it's still baloney."

Al Smith, on campaign promises

"He who slings mud generally loses ground."

Adlai Stevenson

CANADA

"A great guy socially—that is, for someone who turned Canada into a socialist country."

Harold Ballard, hockey owner, on Pierre Trudeau

"Well, I lie all the time. I have to—to balance the family ticket."

> *Lillian Carter, on her son Jimmy*
> *saying he would never lie to the*
> *American people*

"The last time I worked for a president I got one to three years."

> *Charles Colson, former Nixon aide,*
> *on working with Jimmy Carter in*
> *Habitat for Humanity*

"I don't know what people have against Jimmy Carter. He's done nothing."

> *Bob Hope, campaigning for Ronald*
> *Reagan against Carter*

"You know what kind of competitor he is? When he beats me, the entire world should know. When I beat him, it's a national secret."

> *Hamilton Jordan, on playing tennis*
> *with Jimmy Carter*

"Carter was the first politician in memory to come complete with halo."

> *Morris Udall, on Carter's angelic image during the '76 presidential campaign*

CELEBRITY

"The nice thing about being a celebrity is that when you bore people, they think it's their fault."
Henry Kissinger

"Glory is fleeting, but obscurity is forever."
Napoleon

NEVILLE CHAMBERLAIN

"In the depths of that dusty soul is nothing but abject surrender."

> *Winston Churchill, on Chamberlain*

"I have often been accused of putting my foot in my mouth, but I will never put my hands in your pocket."

Spiro Agnew

"An honest politician is one who, when he is bought, will stay bought."

Simon Cameron

"Only lie about the future."

Johnny Carson, advice to politicians

"There are no friends at cards or world politics."

Finley Peter Dunne

"If we don't get Treen out of office soon, there won't be any money left to steal."

Edwin Edwards, on running for governor of Louisiana against David Treen

"Politics is an excellent career, unless you get caught."

> *Robert Half*

"Never judge a country by its politics. After all, we English are quite honest by nature, aren't we?"

> *Alfred Hitchcock*

"You can't adopt politics as a profession and remain honest."

> *Louis McHenry Howe, U.S. diplomat*

"Now and then an innocent man is sent to the legislature."

> *Kin Hubbard*

"Whenever a man has cast a longing eye on offices, a rottenness begins in his conduct."

> *Thomas Jefferson*

"Instead of giving a politician the keys to the city, it might be better to change the locks."

> *Doug Larsen*

"Sooner or later all politicians die of swallowing their own lies."
> *Clare Boothe Luce*

"When buying and selling are controlled by legislators, the first things to be bought and sold are legislators."
> *P. J. O'Rourke*

"Public office is the last refuge of a scoundrel."
> *Boies Penrose, Pennsylvania senator*

"Once a man holds public office he is absolutely no good for honest work."
> *Will Rogers*

"If they ever injected truth into politics, you'd have no politics."
> *Will Rogers*

"You can fool too many of the people too much of the time."
> *James Thurber*

CHINA

"I think you would have to agree, Mr. Secretary, that this is a great wall."

> *Richard Nixon, said to Secretary of State William Rogers about the Great Wall of China*

WINSTON CHURCHILL

"It's fun to be in the same decade with you."

> *Franklin Roosevelt, to Churchill*

CIA

"The CIA is made up of boys whose families sent them to Princeton but wouldn't let them into the family brokerage business."

> *Lyndon Johnson*

"Bill Clinton is just the opposite of Will Rogers. He never met a woman he didn't like."
Joey Adams

"Say what you want about the President, but we know his friends have convictions."
Dick Armey

"Ronald Reagan has a story for every occasion. Bill Clinton has an excuse."
Fred Barnes

"If Bill Clinton is an 8-handicap, I'm Bobby Jones."
George Bush, on Clinton's claim he was an 8-handicap

"I forgive him, since I know the frailty of human nature. He has such a tremendous personality that I think the ladies just go wild over him."
Reverend Billy Graham

"Shaking hands with Bill Clinton is, in and of itself, a full-body sexual experience, I promise you. He has the sexiest handshake of any man that I have ever experienced in my life."

Judith Krantz, author

"The President bought six books at a local bookstore. I guess he didn't want to be seen at the checkout counter with just the Cindy Crawford calendar."

Jay Leno, on President Clinton's activities during a vacation

"I think most of us learned a long time ago that if you don't like the President's position on a particular issue, you simply need to wait a few weeks."

David Obey

"We elected him president, not pope."

Barbra Streisand, on the alleged affairs of the President

"Ronnie's hero is Calvin Coolidge and Nancy's is Calvin Klein."

> *Bob Hope, on the Reagans*

"He has $50 neckties and $400 suits. A $400 suit on old Uncle Earl would look like socks on a rooster."

> *Earl Long, comparing his style of clothes to that of New Orleans mayor deLesseps Morrison*

"I think I'm too expensive for her. She's a Democrat, and it's more than she would normally want to spend."

> *Sara Phillips, designer of Hillary Clinton's inaugural outfit, on the First Lady's reluctance to purchase more clothes from Phillips in the early years of the administration*

COMMON SENSE

"If a man has good common sense, he has about all the sense there is."

Sam Rayburn

COMMUNISM

"Any pitcher who throws at a batter and deliberately tries to hurt him is a Communist."

Alvin Dark, former major-league baseball player

"I'd get me a bunch of bats and balls and sneak me a couple of umpires and learn the kids behind the Iron Curtain how to take a bat and play baseball."

Dizzy Dean, on how to stop Communism

"Eisenhower told me never to trust a Communist."

Lyndon Johnson

"Communism is like Prohibition. It's a good idea, but it won't work."
Will Rogers

CONGRESS

"You can't use tact with a congressman. A congressman is a hog. You must take a stick and hit him on the snout."
Henry Adams

"Open each session with a prayer and close it with a probe."
Clarence Brown, Ohio congressman

"If $120,000 a year is the best job you ever had, you haven't really done very much."
Tom Clancy, on the problem with Congress

"We have leadership—there's just no fellowship."
George Danielson, California congressman, on leadership in Congress

"A constitutional right, when elected to Congress, is to be a damn fool and act like one."

William Ford, Michigan congressman,
on being elected to Congress

"We have the power to do any damn fool thing we want to do, and we seem to do it about every ten minutes."

William Fulbright

"The only way to get anywhere in Congress is to stay there and let seniority take its course."

John Nance Garner

"Talk is cheap—except when Congress does it."

Cullen Hightower

"The mistakes made by Congress wouldn't be so bad if the next Congress didn't keep trying to correct them."

Cullen Hightower

"Congress."

Lyndon Johnson, asked his handicap
when he showed up at the Masters

"They say if we give them a 50 percent pay increase they'll stop outside speaking engagements. Maybe if we give them 100 percent, they'll stop talking altogether."

Jay Leno, on congressional pay raises

"There are two periods when Congress does no business: one is before the holidays, and the other after."

George Prentice

"The most delicious of all privileges—spending other people's money."

John Randolph, on serving in Congress

"Congress is the highest theater that anyone plays in upon this earth today."

Sam Rayburn

"The gentleman need not worry. He will never be either."

Thomas Reed, responding to a congressman who paraphrased Henry Clay by saying he would rather be right than be president

"The way to judge a good comedy is by how long it will last and how people talk about it. Now, Congress has turned out some that have lived for years and people are still laughing about them."

Will Rogers

"When the Congress makes a law, it's a joke; and when the Congress makes a joke, it's the law."

Will Rogers

"They are just children that never grew up. They don't like to be corrected in company. Don't send messages to 'em, send candy."

Will Rogers, advice to FDR on handling Congress

"Rail splitting produced an unparalleled president in Abraham Lincoln, but golf hasn't produced even a good A-1 congressman."

Will Rogers

"There is no credit to being a comedian when you have the whole government working for you. All you have to do is report the facts. I don't even have to exaggerate."

Will Rogers

"Never blame a legislative body for not doing something. When they do nothing, that doesn't hurt anybody. When they do something is when they become dangerous."

Will Rogers

"Congress does from a third to half of what I think is the minimum that it ought to do, and I am profoundly grateful that I get as much."

Theodore Roosevelt

"Give a member of Congress a junket and a mimeograph machine and he thinks he is secretary of state."

Dean Rusk

"I'm the only member here who hasn't broken both arms by patting myself on the back."

Pete Stark, California congressman, on the 1998–99 budget agreement

"All congresses and parliaments have a kindly feeling for idiots and a compassion to them on account of personal experience and heredity."

Mark Twain

"Fleas can be taught anything that a congressman can."

> Mark Twain

"If you don't know one of these new fellas, just call him Mr. Chairman and you're safe."

> Morris Udall, on all the congressional committees and subcommittees that have been created over the years

"Congress in session is Congress on public exhibition, whilst Congress in its committee rooms is Congress at work."

> Woodrow Wilson

CONSENSUS

"When two men agree on everything, one of them is doing all the thinking."

> Sam Rayburn

CONSERVATIVES

"A conservative is a person who comes to Bentonville, Arkansas, to study Wal-Mart and learn how to fix the post office. A liberal is a person who comes to Bentonville, Arkansas, to make Wal-Mart like the post office."
Newt Gingrich

"Many Americans don't like the simple things. That's what they have against conservatives."
Barry Goldwater

"A conservative: one who is opposed to the things he is in favor of."
Elbert Hubbard

"Some fellows get credit for being conservative when they are only stupid."
Elbert Hubbard

"What is conservative? Is it not adherence to the old and tried against the new and untried?"
Abraham Lincoln

"A conservative is a liberal who was mugged the night before."

Frank Rizzo

"A conservative is a man who just thinks and sits, mostly sits."

Woodrow Wilson

CONSTITUENTS

"The best audience is intelligent, well educated, and a little drunk."

Alben Barkley

"A political leader must keep looking over his shoulder all the time to see if the boys are still there. If they aren't still there, he's no longer a political leader."

Bernard Baruch

CONSTITUTION

"The American Constitution is, so far as I can see, the most wonderful work ever struck off at a given time by the brain and purpose of man."
William Gladstone

CONVENTIONS

"It wasn't my finest hour. It wasn't even my finest hour and a half."

> *Bill Clinton, after giving an endless nominating speech for Michael Dukakis at the '88 Democratic convention*

"A chess tournament disguised as a circus."
Alistair Cooke, defining a convention

"A rigged convention is one with the other man's delegates in control. An open convention is when your delegates are in control."
James Farley

"I stayed up late last night and watched the Republican convention all night long. I watched all of the talk and listened to them and saw them, and I'm not interested in politics. If you watch them and listen to them, you can find out why you're not."

Casey Stengel

CALVIN COOLIDGE

"I think the American people want a solemn ass as a president. And I think I'll go along with them."

Calvin Coolidge, on why he was seeking the presidency

"One of the most important accomplishments of my administration has been minding my own business."

Calvin Coolidge

"Calvin Coolidge is the greatest man who ever came out of Plymouth, Vermont."

Clarence Darrow

"I do wish he did not look as if he had been weaned on a pickle."

Alice Roosevelt Longworth

"A remarkable man, a really remarkable man. Nero fiddles while Rome burned, but Coolidge only snores."

H. L. Mencken

"How could they tell?"

Dorothy Parker, after being told that former president Coolidge had died

CRIMES AND MISDEMEANORS

"Obviously crime pays, or there'd be no crime."
G. Gordon Liddy

"A good politician is quite as unthinkable as an honest burglar."

H. L. Mencken

"When the President does it, that means it's not illegal."

Richard Nixon

"We do many things at the federal level that would be considered dishonest and illegal if done in the private sector."

Donald Regan

"When they call the roll in the Senate, the senators do not know whether to answer 'present' or 'not guilty.'"

Theodore Roosevelt

"No people is fully civilized where a distinction is drawn between stealing an office and stealing a purse."

Theodore Roosevelt

CRISS

"Next week there can't be any crisis. My schedule is already full."

Henry Kissinger

CRITICS

"A thick skin is a gift from God."
Konrad Adenauer

"My daddy told me that if I didn't want to get shot at, I should stay out of the firing line. This is politics."
Lyndon Johnson

"If I sought to answer all of the criticisms that cross my desk, my secretaries would be engaged in little else."
Martin Luther King, Jr.

"So many people want me to be apologetic, I'm beginning to refer to myself as Mayor Culpa."
Ed Koch, on being blamed for many things as mayor

"When they're after your butt, answer the phone."
Alan Simpson, advice to Hillary Clinton on fighting back at critics

"I am calling this budget the Charlie Brown budget, because all we are getting back is peanuts."

> *Glenn Liebman, executive director, Alliance for the Mentally Ill of New York State, on the 1997–98 New York State budget for mental health*

"Even though they're in a hurry, the Republicans have not forgotten their manners. When it comes to cutting benefits, it's still women and children first."

> *Bill Maher, said just prior to a congressional recess*

"If you can't fill the till, don't pass the bill."

> *Ann Richards, on the fiscal implications of signing bills*

"If the rest of Washington ran as efficiently as this football team, there wouldn't be any deficit."

Jeff Bostic, on the NFL's Washington Redskins during their good years

"The farther you get away from Washington, the more you think that things are under control there."

Art Buchwald

"There are a number of things wrong with Washington. One of them is that everyone has been too long away from home."

Dwight Eisenhower

"I came to Washington, D.C., like prime steak, and after being here for a while, I feel like poor-grade hamburger."

Joycelyn Elders, former U.S. surgeon general

"No matter what you do, be honest. That stands out in Washington."

Barry Goldwater

"The really scary thing is that some of these people work for the government."

> *Joe Jacoby, on Redskins fans who show up for games wearing pig snouts*

"Washington is Salem. If we're not lynching somebody twenty-four hours a day in this wretched town, we're not happy."

> *Tom Korologos, lobbyist*

"Washington is a place where politicians don't know which way is up and taxes don't know which way is down."

> *Robert Obren*

"The mystery of government is not how Washington works but how to make it stop."

> *P. J. O'Rourke*

"People only leave by way of the box—ballot or coffin."

> *Claiborne Pell, on how people leave Washington*

"The District of Columbia is one gigantic ear."
Ronald Reagan

"Washington is a very easy city for you to forget where you came from and why you got there in the first place."
Harry Truman

DEBATES

"Why do Republicans fear debate? For the same reason baloney fears the slicer."
Lloyd Bentsen, vice-presidential candidate in 1988, elaborating on his claim that the Republicans were refusing to debate

"They never open their mouths without subtracting from the sum of human knowledge."
Thomas Reed, on two congressmen who constantly debated each other

"A good catchword can obscure analysis for fifty years."
Wendell Willkie, on debating

DEBT

"Blessed are the young, for they shall inherit the national debt."

Herbert Hoover

DECISIONS

"People say I'm indecisive, but I don't know about that."

George Bush, poking fun at himself

"I may not know enough about being president, but I do know that a lot of decisions can be made on golf courses."

Warren Harding

DEFENSE

"That's more than the Clinton administration is spending on arms."

>*Don McMillan, on the Atlanta Braves' signing all three of their star pitchers to long-term contracts*

"The President says the defense budget is not sacrosanct. That means they are laying off six waiters from the Army-Navy game."

>*Mark Russell*

DEMOCRACY

"Democracy is the worst system developed by the wit of man, except for all the others."

>*Winston Churchill*

"Democracy means that if the doorbell rings in the early hours, it is likely to be the milkman."

>*Winston Churchill*

"The world is weary of statesmen whom democracy has degraded into politicians."
Benjamin Disraeli

"Democracy is like a raft. It won't sink, but you'll always have your feet wet."
Russell Long

"Democracy is that art of running the circus from the monkey cage."
H. L. Mencken

"I confess I enjoy democracy immensely. It is incomparably idiotic and . . . incomparably amusing."
H. L. Mencken

"Democracy may not prove in the long run to be as efficient as other forms of government, but it has one saving grace: it allows us to know and say that it isn't."
Bill Moyers

"In a democracy things happen by leadership or by crisis."
Leon Panetta

"Democracy substitutes selection by the incompetent many for appointment by the corrupt few."

George Bernard Shaw

"All the ills of democracy can be cured by more democracy."

Alfred Smith

DEMOCRATS

"Listening to Democrats complain about inflation is like listening to germs complain about disease."

Spiro Agnew

"All men are democrats when they are happy."

G. K. Chesterton

"The Democratic party ain't on speaking terms with itself."

Finley Peter Dunne

"Well, I was raised a Democrat."

*Jerry Falwell, asked if he had any
hidden scandals in his past*

"I never said all Democrats were saloon keepers.
What I said was that all saloon keepers are
Democrats."

Horace Greeley

"The Democratic party at its worst is better for the
country than the Republican party at its best."

Lyndon Johnson

"I suppose if I was offered enough money I'd try
the pros. Everybody has his price. For enough
money, I'd become a Communist. Well, maybe not
a Communist. A Democrat, anyway."

*Abe Lemons, college basketball coach,
asked if he would consider coaching
in the NBA*

"Have you ever tried to split sawdust?"

*Eugene McCarthy, asked if his
running for president in 1968 would
split the Democratic party*

"You have to have been a Republican to know how good it is to be a Democrat."

Jackie Kennedy Onassis

"A party of doom and gloom."

Dan Quayle, on the Democrats

"You can never underestimate the ability of the Democrats to wet their finger and hold it to the wind."

Ronald Reagan

"The Democratic party is like a horse driving backward in a railroad car—it never sees anything until it has got past it."

Thomas Reed, Republican congressman

"This is the first time I have received an invitation to the Democratic headquarters."

Thomas Reed, Republican congressman, after being told by a heckler to go to hell

"The Democratic party is like a mule without pride of ancestry or hope of posterity."

Emory Speer, Georgia congressman

"The difference between a national Democrat and an Alabama Democrat is like the difference between a Communist and a non-Communist."

George Wallace

DEMONSTRATIONS

"A riot is at bottom the language of the unheard."

Martin Luther King, Jr.

DESERT STORM

"It's going to be a war out there. I just don't know if we're going to be the United States or Kuwait."

Charles Barkley, on the Philadelphia 76ers' prospects for 1992

"In light of the Gulf crisis, we thought a brunette was more appropriate."

> *Tina Brown, former editor of* Vanity
> Fair, *on putting Cher instead of*
> *Marla Maples on the cover during the*
> *Gulf War*

"These damned drums are keeping me up all night."

> *George Bush, on antiwar protesters*
> *playing drums outside the White*
> *House during the Gulf War*

"Why do we feel good? Because the big gorilla whipped a midget."

> *Ross Perot, on the Gulf War*

DIPLOMACY

"Diplomacy. The patriotic act of lying for one's country."

> *Ambrose Bierce*

"American diplomacy is easy on the brain but hell on the feet."

Charles Dawes

"The chief distinction of a diplomat is that he can say no in such a way that it sounds like yes."

Lester Bowles Pearson, former Canadian prime minister

"A diplomat's life is made up of three ingredients— protocol, Geritol, and alcohol."

Adlai Stevenson

DOG—EAT—DOG WORLD

"My dog Millie knows more about foreign affairs than those two bozos."

George Bush, on the foreign-policy experience of Bill Clinton and Al Gore

"Elizabeth's back at the Red Cross and I'm walking the dog."

> *Bob Dole, on his retirement activities*
> *after losing the '96 presidential*
> *election*

"What counts is not necessarily the size of the dog in the fight—it's the size of the fight in the dog."
> *Dwight Eisenhower*

"This is the kindest cut of all."
> *Wayne Pacelle, Humane Society,*
> *after President Clinton's dog Buddy*
> *was neutered*

"If you want a friend in this life, get a dog."
> *Harry Truman*

ROBERT DOLE

"Look, I won! I'm back."
> *Bob Dole, on the press corps camped*
> *outside the Watergate apartment*
> *where Monica Lewinsky lived, a few*
> *doors down from Dole*

"Dole should be beatable. Even I beat him."

> *Walter Mondale, on Clinton's chances against Dole*

"It's Dole's misfortune that when he does smile, he looks as if he's just evicted a widow."

> *Mike Royko*

"He's married to the head of the American Red Cross, so he can get fresh blood whenever he wants."

> *Harry Shearer, on why Dole's age and health should not have been a factor against Clinton*

DOONESBURY

"I wouldn't have invited me either."

> *Garry Trudeau, on not being invited to a luncheon for political cartoonists with President Reagan*

DRINKING

"The reason there are two senators from each state is so that one can be the designated driver."
   Jay Leno

"The Lord looks after drunks and Americans."
   Daniel Patrick Moynihan, on why no Americans were killed during the invasion of Haiti

MICHAEL DUKAKIS

"Michael Dukakis thinks a foreign market is a place to go for French bread."
   Rich Bond, adviser to President Bush, on Dukakis's lack of foreign-policy experience

JOHN FOSTER DULLES

"The only bull I know who carries his own china closet with him."

Winston Churchill, describing Dulles

ECONOMISTS

"Economics is extremely useful as a form of employment for economists."

John Kenneth Galbraith

"Economist—a man who states the obvious in terms of the incomprehensible."

Alfred Knopf

"To me this is a kind of sad profession, although it is the only profession where you can gain great eminence without ever being right."

George Meany

"Oh yeah, I remember him—shortstop, mustache, plays third base for Pittsburgh."

Jackie Moore, baseball manager,
when told he was on the same plane
as economist John Kenneth Galbraith

"A friend of mine was asked to a costume ball a short time ago. He slapped some egg on his face and went as a liberal economist."

Ronald Reagan

"An economist's guess is liable to be just as good as anybody else's."

Will Rogers

"If all economists were laid end to end, they would not reach a conclusion."

George Bernard Shaw

"I was in search of a one-armed economist so that the guy could never make a statement and then say, 'on the other hand.'"

Harry Truman

ECONOMY

"I feel like a mosquito in a nudist colony. The real question is where to strike first."

> *Phil Gramm, on Clinton's economic policy*

"I learned more about economics from one South Dakota dust storm than I did in all my years in college."

> *Hubert Humphrey*

"Every bright spot the White House finds in the economy is like the policeman bending over the body in the alley and saying cheerfully, 'Two wounds are fatal. The other one is not so bad.'"

> *John F. Kennedy, on the Eisenhower administration's rosy economic forecasts*

"Politicians say they're beefing up our economy. Most don't know beef from pork."

> *Harold Lowman*

"Recession is when a neighbor loses his job, depression is when you lose yours, and recovery is when Jimmy Carter loses his job."

Ronald Reagan, said during the '80 presidential campaign

"The nation is prosperous on the whole, but how much prosperity is there in a hole?"

Will Rogers

EDUCATION

"I never graduated from the University of Iowa, but I was only there for two terms—Truman's and Eisenhower's."

Alex Karras, former professional football player

"A man who has never gone to school may steal from a freight car. But if he has a university education, he may steal the whole railroad."

Theodore Roosevelt

EGO

"He that falls in love with himself will have no rivals."

Benjamin Franklin

"You have to do a little bragging on yourself even to your relatives—man doesn't get anywhere without advertising."

John Nance Garner

"I am deeply touched—not as deeply touched as you have been coming to this dinner, but nonetheless it is a sentimental occasion."

John F. Kennedy, during a fund-raising dinner

"The capacity to admire others is not my most fully developed trait."

Henry Kissinger

"Me."

> *Henry Kissinger, asked for* Time *magazine's 75th-anniversary issue to name the person who most shaped public policy since the magazine's founding*

"I want to come back as me."

> *Ed Koch, on reincarnation*

"There are three and a half million Asians who don't know Ed Rollins."

> *Ed Rollins, on deciding to do consulting in Asia after some political problems in the United States*

"All politicians have vanity. Some wear it more gently than others."

> *David Steel, British politician*

"Ben Hogan for President. If we're going to have a golfer, let's have a good one."

> *Anonymous, popular slogan used against Eisenhower, who was an avid golfer*

"Eisenhower isn't a Communist. He's a golfer."

> *Russell Baker, on claims that Eisenhower was soft on Communism*

"It's hard to play a guy who rattles his medals while you're putting."

> *Bob Hope, on playing golf with President Eisenhower*

"Once he makes up his mind, he's full of indecision."

> *Oscar Levant, on President Eisenhower*

"Stick your butt out more."

> *Sam Snead, golf advice he gave to President Eisenhower*

"Golf is a fine release from the tensions of office, but we are a little tired of holding the bag."

> *Adlai Stevenson, on Eisenhower's*
> *love of golf*

"If I talk over people's heads, Ike must talk under their feet."

> *Adlai Stevenson*

"He'll sit there and he'll say, 'Do this! Do that!' and nothing will happen. Poor Ike—it won't be a bit like the army."

> *Harry Truman, on Eisenhower*
> *dealing with the government after a*
> *military career*

ELECTIONS

"What I'm worried about is what I'm going to do if I'm *not* elected."

> *John Allen, Mississippi congressman,*
> *asked what he would do if he were*
> *reelected*

"In every election in American history both parties have their clichés. The party that has the clichés that ring true wins."

Newt Gingrich

"I guess the truth can hurt you worse in an election than about anything that could happen to you."

Will Rogers

"More men have been elected between sundown and sunup than ever were elected between sunup and sundown."

Will Rogers

"You know how it is in an election year. They pick a president and then for four years they pick on him."

Adlai Stevenson

"A candidate has a hard life—he has to shave twice a day."

Adlai Stevenson

"Democracy's ceremonial—its feast, its great function, is the election."
> *H. G. Wells*

"I know nothing grander, better exercise, better digestion, more positive proof of the past, the triumphant result of faith in humankind, than a well-contested American national election."
> *Walt Whitman*

ENEMIES

"It's a damned good thing to remember in politics to stick to your party and never attempt to buy the favor of your enemies at the expense of your friends."
> *Joseph Cannon*

"Those people who have done me wrong—well, I try to outlive them."
> *Happy Chandler, governor of Kentucky, on the best revenge*

"Forgive your enemies, but never forget their names."

>   *John F. Kennedy*

"A friend is one who has the same enemies you have."

>   *Abraham Lincoln*

"A politician knows that his friends are not always his allies and that his adversaries are not his enemies."

>   *Richard Nixon*

"You don't make peace with friends. You make it with very unsavory enemies."

>   *Yitzhak Rabin, Israel's prime minister, on recognition of the PLO*

"Judge me by the enemies I have made."

>   *Franklin Roosevelt*

ENVIRONMENT

"Naming a national forest after Ronald Reagan is like naming a day-care center after W. C. Fields."
> *Bob Mattox, Sierra Club, on a*
> *proposal to name a California*
> *national forest after President*
> *Reagan*

"A tree is a tree—how many more do you need to look at?"
> *Ronald Reagan*

"It is exciting to have a real crisis on your hands when you have spent half your political life dealing with humdrum issues like the environment."
> *Margaret Thatcher, on the Falkland*
> *Islands war*

EXPERTS

"An expert is someone who is capable of articulating the interests of people with power."
> *Henry Kissinger*

"An expert is somebody who is more than fifty miles from home, has no responsibility for implementing the advice he gives, and shows slides."

Ed Meese

"There are as many opinions as there are experts."
Franklin Roosevelt

FACE—TO—FACE

"If there's a plastic surgeon who claims to be responsible for this face, then New York State will decertify him immediately."

Mario Cuomo, responding to claims
he had a face-lift

"If I had another face, do you think I would wear this one?"

Abraham Lincoln, on Stephen
Douglas calling him two-faced

"It's been a long time since either one of us have gone out of each other's way to contact the other."
> *Roger Clinton, on his relationship with Hillary Clinton*

"No, I can beat him already."
> *Jack Ford, asked if he was getting tennis advice from then-girlfriend Chris Evert on how to beat his dad, President Ford*

"They're in a high enough income-tax bracket where most of them start thinking Republican."
> *Jeff Kemp, former Seattle Seahawks quarterback, on getting support from teammates for his dad Jack's presidential campaign*

"If you have 30 cousins, it's pretty easy."
> *Joe Kennedy II, on fund-raising for his first congressional campaign*

"He could pick up his clothes a little more."

> *Marilyn Quayle, on how she would change her husband Dan for the better*

"I can do one of two things. I can be president of the United States or I can control Alice. I cannot possibly do both."

> *Theodore Roosevelt, on his outspoken daughter Alice*

"I have found the best way to give advice to your children is to find out what they want and then advise them to do it."

> *Harry Truman*

FANATICS

"A fanatic is one who can't change his mind and won't change the subject."

> *Winston Churchill*

FARMS

"Raise less corn and more hell."

> *Mary Elizabeth Lease, on farmers in the 1890s being forced into foreclosure*

"I grew up on a farm, and I might say that my visit to the Oval Office for lunch with the President was more in the nature of a visit to the woodshed after supper."

> *David Stockman, former Reagan budget director, after being criticized for revealing some controversial opinions about the budget process*

FIRST LADIES

"As you know, we have a lot in common. She adores her husband, I adore mine. She fights drugs, I fight illiteracy. She wears a size three . . . so's my leg."

> *Barbara Bush, contrasting her style with that of Nancy Reagan*

"I got away with murder. I'm now more careful about what I say. Slightly."

> *Barbara Bush, on the difference between being Second Lady and First Lady*

"You'd think he was running for First Lady."

> *Bill Clinton, on George Bush's criticism of Hillary Clinton*

"The one thing I do not want to be called is First Lady. It sounds like a saddle horse."

> *Jackie Kennedy*

"Being First Lady is the hardest unpaid job in the world."

> *Pat Nixon*

"He listened, but he does have a mind of his own."

> *Nancy Reagan, comparing her role as adviser to her husband to that of Hillary Clinton*

"Until you've lived through a White House Easter egg hunt, you don't know what hell is."

Merrie Spaeth, aide to Nancy Reagan, offering advice to Hillary Clinton

FIRST MEN

"I can trust my husband not to fall asleep on a public platform, and he usually claps in the right places."

Margaret Thatcher, on the role of her husband

FLAG

"Many a bum show has been saved by the flag."
George M. Cohan

"I felt like I was punching the American flag."
Al Smith, hockey player, on fighting with 1980 U.S. gold medal Olympic hero Jim Craig

"If you want a symbolic gesture, don't burn the flag—wash it."

Norman Thomas

FLATTERY

"Flattery is all right—if you don't have to inhale."
Adlai Stevenson

"You spoke so flatteringly about me that for a moment I thought I was dead."

Harry Truman, on praise he received from Israeli ambassador Abba Eban

FLY THE FRIENDLY SKIES

"Sorry about the crowding, but welcome to coach class."

Mike DeWine, Ohio senator, to seven airline heads forced to sit in close quarters while testifying about antitrust legislation

"**M**rs. Clinton, all we are saying is give peas a chance."

> *Tom Brokaw, on Hillary Clinton's dislike of peas and her failure to mention them during a* Sesame Street *show on vegetables*

"**W**e've made a lot of progress on, you know, pasta and things like that—but tofu has been hard for us."

> *Hillary Clinton, on improving President Clinton's diet*

"**F**or once Rush can't be accused of not knowing what he's talking about."

> *Jay Leno, on Rush Limbaugh doing commercials for Pizza Hut*

"**I**t's ugly in there. Food is flying all over the place."

> *Mike McCurry, to the press corps while President Clinton and German chancellor Helmut Kohl were sharing a huge meal*

"When she's not on board, we chow down."
> Brian Williams, on Hillary Clinton,
> who often urges everyone to eat
> healthy food when she is on Air Force
> One

"Not enough salt in the hamburger."
> Boris Yeltsin, after eating a
> hamburger at a new McDonald's in
> Moscow

FOOTBALL

"The Miami offense can really bomb you. They must get their players from Lebanon or the Middle East somewhere."
> Bobby Bowden, on the offense of the
> University of Miami football team

"I always enjoy animal acts."
> Calvin Coolidge, asked if he would
> like to meet some members of the
> Chicago Bears

"Pro football gave me a great sense of perspective to enter politics. I'd already been booed, cheered, cut, sold, traded, and hung in effigy."
Jack Kemp

"Politics is an astonishing profession. It has enabled me to go from being an obscure member of the junior varsity at Harvard to being an honorary member of the Football Hall of Fame."
John F. Kennedy

"Politics is like football. If you see daylight, go through the hole."
John F. Kennedy

"Being in politics is like being a football coach. You have to be smart enough to know the game and stupid enough to think it's important."
Eugene McCarthy

"We're 28 Republicans who vote socialist."
Art Modell, football owner, on how the NFL shares television revenue and gate receipts

"If you would turn them over to us, we'd put them in silos and we wouldn't have to build the MX missile."

> *Ronald Reagan, on the Oakland Raiders*

"In life, as in a football game, the principle to follow is: Hit the line hard, don't foul and don't shirk, but hit the line hard."

> *Theodore Roosevelt*

"It's a lot tougher to be a football coach than a president. You've got four years as president, and they guard you. A coach doesn't have anyone to protect him when things go wrong."

> *Harry Truman*

BETTY FORD

"My wife is much more interesting."

> *Gerald Ford, when asked why they were doing a movie about his wife's life and not his*

"Whenever I play with him, I usually try to make it a foursome—the President, myself, a paramedic, and a faith healer."

> *Bob Hope, on the erratic golf game*
> *of President Ford*

"We have 51 golf courses in Palm Springs. He never decides which course he usually plays until after his first tee shot."

> *Bob Hope, on President Ford*

"He plays such a great game of golf for a guy wearing skis."

> *Bob Hope, on President Ford's love of*
> *skiing*

"Gerald Ford is a nice guy, but he played too much football with his helmet off."

> *Lyndon Johnson*

"First, hitting the ball—second, finding out where it went."

> *Tom Watson, golf advice to President*
> *Ford*

FOREIGN POLICY

"Do not criticize your government when out of the country. Never cease to do so when at home."
Winston Churchill

"We cannot play innocents abroad in a world that is not innocent."
Ronald Reagan, on foreign policy

"In foreign policy you have to wait 25 years to see how it comes out."
James Reston

"Foreign relations is an open book—generally a checkbook."
Will Rogers

"Making foreign policy is a little bit like making pornographic movies. It's more fun doing it than watching it."
William Rogers, former secretary of state

FRANCE

"If it were not for the government, we should have nothing left to laugh at in France."
Nicolas Chamfort

"When I want to know what France thinks, I ask myself."
Charles de Gaulle

"How can you be expected to govern a country that has 246 kinds of cheeses?"
Charles de Gaulle

MOHANDAS GANDHI

"Generations to come . . . will scarce believe that such a one as this ever walked upon this earth."
Albert Einstein

JOHN NANCE GARNER

"A poker-playing, whiskey-drinking, evil old man."
John L. Lewis, on Garner

GAYS IN THE MILITARY

"You don't need to be straight to die for your country. You just need to shoot straight."
Barry Goldwater

"Wouldn't you want me on the front lines?"
Martina Navratilova, on gays in the military

GET OUT THE VOTE

"Vote for the man who promises least. He'll be the least disappointing."
Bernard Baruch

"Vote: the instrument and symbol of a freeman's power to make a fool of himself and a wreck of his country."

Ambrose Bierce

"The most important political office is that of private citizen."

Louis Brandeis

"I never vote for anybody—I always vote against."

W. C. Fields

"Constantly choosing the lesser of two evils is still choosing evil."

Jerry Garcia, on voting

"Harry had won by such a narrow margin he might not have made it if Bess hadn't voted for her husband."

Bob Hope, on Harry Truman
narrowly defeating Thomas Dewey

"We'd all like to vote for the best man, but he's never a candidate."

Kin Hubbard

"In politics, familiarity doesn't breed contempt. It breeds voters."

Paul Lazarsfeld, sociologist

"It's very close, but I'd take Bush. I want him to win because he's a tennis player."

Ilie Nastase, on his picking Bush over Dukakis in the '88 presidential election

"It's not enough. I need a majority."

Adlai Stevenson, when told he would get the vote of every thinking man in the United States

"It's not the hand that signs the law that holds the destiny of America. It's the hand that casts the ballot."

Harry Truman

"Whenever a fella tells me he's bipartisan, I know he's going to vote against me."

Harry Truman

"It's not just because he didn't invite me to dinner, but because on my way into town from the airport there were such enormous potholes."

> *Fidel Castro, on why he would never vote for Rudy Giuliani, mayor of New York City*

"A tennis player asked Rudy for advice, and he said, 'Take two and hit to right.' He doesn't understand anything about tennis."

> *David Dinkins, former mayor of New York City*

GOD BLESS THE USA

"America is the only country in the world where you can go on the air and kid politicians—and where politicians go on the air and kid the people."

> *Groucho Marx*

"Think of what would happen to us in America if there were no humorists; life would be one long *Congressional Record.*"
                    Tom Masson

"The saving grace of America lies in the fact that the overwhelming majority of Americans are possessed of two qualities—a sense of humor and a sense of proportion."
                    Franklin Roosevelt

"A man who thinks of himself as belonging to a particular national group in America has not yet become an American."
                    Woodrow Wilson

"It is the only place where miracles not only happen, but where they happen all the time."
                    Thomas Wolfe, on the United States

"It may be of value to the golf fan who plans to attend the next Bob Hope Desert Classic—I know that I intend to participate. Check the guest list before you venture out."

> *Spiro Agnew, after hitting two fans*
> *in a row at the Desert Classic*

"As if we don't have enough violence on television."

> *Barbara Bush, on watching her*
> *husband and Presidents Ford and*
> *Clinton golf at the Bob Hope Classic*

"Well, for one thing, I find that I no longer win every golf game I play."

> *George Bush, on how he is treated*
> *after his presidency*

"Golf is a game whose sole aim is to hit a very small ball into an even smaller hole, with weapons singularly ill designed for that purpose."

> *Winston Churchill*

"When I get home I'm going to have to try to bribe President Bush and get a set of his."

> Roger Clemens, on being outbid for a set of John F. Kennedy's golf clubs

"I've got a new idea. Try the fairway."

> Bill Clinton, after one of his golf partners hit a lousy shot

"The best perks of this office are who you get to play golf with. I've played with Jack Nicklaus, Arnold Palmer, Raymond Floyd, Amy Alcott."

> Bill Clinton

"It was hot. I was smokin' 'em. Even a blind pig finds an acorn sometimes."

> Bill Clinton, after shooting a 79

"Playing the game, I have learned the meaning of humility. It has given me an understanding of the futility of the human effort."

> Abba Eban

"You have to let a little air into the war room now and then."

Dwight Eisenhower, on his love of golf

"I just loaned Bolivia $2 million, but I play $1 Nassaus."

Dwight Eisenhower

"There ought to be a law against asking a golfer what he shoots."

Dwight Eisenhower

"It is a sport in which the whole American family can participate—fathers and mothers, sons and daughters alike. It offers healthy respite from daily toil, refreshment of body and mind."

Dwight Eisenhower

"The pat on the back, the arm around the shoulder, the praise for what was done right, and the sympathetic nod for what wasn't are as much a part of golf as life itself."

Gerald Ford

"Don't ever walk in front of them."

> *Scott Hoch, pro golfer, on what he*
> *learned after playing golf with*
> *several presidents*

"Hit till you're happy."

> *Lyndon Johnson, summarizing his*
> *golf strategy*

"It is true that my predecessor did not object as I do to pictures of one's golfing shots in action. But neither, on the other hand, did he ever bean a Secret Service agent."

> *John F. Kennedy*

"I tried my level best to make Calvin Coolidge president."

> *Ring Lardner, after almost hitting*
> *President Harding with a shot at a*
> *golf tournament*

"The greatest thrill of my life—even better than getting elected."

> *Richard Nixon, on a hole in one*

"I'm awfully sorry, honey, but I'd have had 30 more yards if you had gotten out of the way."

Tip O'Neill, after hitting a woman on the backside while playing golf

"If I swing the gavel the way I swing a golf club, no wonder the nation's in a mess."

Tip O'Neill

"Is it public? You can get starting times in seven different languages."

Tip O'Neill, when asked if a golf course named after him was public

"Photographs of me on horseback, yes; tennis, no. And golf is fatal."

Theodore Roosevelt

"Golf is a game for people who are not active enough for baseball."

William Howard Taft

AL GORE

"Al Gore is so boring, his Secret Service code name is Al Gore."
Al Gore, on his image

"That means he's busy eating fast food, chasing women, and giving Bob Dole the finger."
David Letterman, on Gore replacing President Clinton while Clinton was on vacation

"I'm going through eye-exercise therapy, strengthening my eyes. I'm supposed to . . . rest them."
Martha Stewart, on her eyes being closed during an Al Gore speech

GUN CONTROL

"It's too bad Moses is so wrong on this one."
Nita Lowey, congresswoman from New York, on Charlton Heston's opposition to gun control

ALEXANDER HAIG

"I don't even know what his constituency is, unless it's retired Army officers."

> *John Anderson, on Alexander Haig*
> *running for president*

HAIL TO THE CHIEF

"More important than the president of the United States."

> *Muhammad Ali, on being the*
> *heavyweight champion*

"I'd rather be a Yankee catcher than president, and that makes me pretty lucky, I guess, because I could never be the president."

> *Yogi Berra*

"The greased pig in the field game of American politics."

> *Ambrose Bierce, on the presidency*

"Anybody that wants the presidency so much that he'll spend two years organizing and campaigning for it is not to be trusted with the office."
David Broder

"I would rather be right than president."
Henry Clay

"When I was a boy I was told that anybody could become president. I'm beginning to believe it."
Clarence Darrow

"There is one thing about being president—nobody can tell you when to sit down."
Dwight Eisenhower

"The second office of this government is honorable and easy. The first is but a splendid misery."
Thomas Jefferson

"Being president is like being a jackass in a hailstorm. There's nothing to do but stand there and take it."
Lyndon Johnson

"Sometimes I wish I just had a summer job here."
John F. Kennedy

"When we got into office the thing that surprised us most was to find that things were just as bad as we'd been saying they were."
John F. Kennedy

"The pay is good and I can walk to work."
John F. Kennedy

"I have been told I was on the road to hell, but I had no idea it was just a mile down the road with a dome on it."
Abraham Lincoln

"Sometimes it seems that I'm a juggler with at least 15 balls in the air and one hand is tied behind my back."
Ronald Reagan

"I would leave the country if I were president."
Sylvester Stallone

"When you get to be president, there are all those things: the honors, and 21-gun salutes, all those things. You have to remember it isn't for you. It's for the presidency."

Harry Truman

"He's the only lobbyist that all the 160 million people in the country have."

Harry Truman

"Any American who is prepared to run for president should automatically, by definition, be disqualified from ever doing so."

Gore Vidal

"The doctor asked me the day of the week and I said 'Friday.' Then he asked me who was the president of the United States and I said, 'Hell, I didn't know that before I hit my head.'"

Don Zimmer, former major-league baseball player, on being beaned in the head

HAIR IT IS

"I call it the Watergate—I cover up everything I can."

Joe Torre, on his hairstyle

"It's all part of reinventing government—he wants 20 percent less hair."

*Lorraine Voles, Al Gore spokesperson,
on his bald spot*

WARREN HARDING

"His speeches leave the impression of an army of pompous phrases moving over the landscape in search of an idea."

William McAdoo, on Harding

BENJAMIN HARRISON

"As glacial as a Siberian stripped of his fur."
> *Tom Platt, the legendary Boss of*
> *New York City, on Benjamin*
> *Harrison's personality*

HART ATTACK

"Some critics complain that Gary Hart doesn't have any experience in foreign policy. But that's not true. Why, just yesterday he had breakfast at the International House of Pancakes."
> *George Bush*

"This is a documentary of my campaign."
> *Gary Hart, holding a copy of* Dumbo
> *at a video store, on his '88*
> *presidential run*

"I don't know if the presidential candidates are running for the White House or Animal House."
> *Bob Hope, on the Hart campaign for*
> *president*

"If he has to talk about price supports, talk corn or soybeans—never mention rice."

Robert Squier, adviser to Gary Hart, on the Donna Rice scandal

HARVARD YARD

"I'll never get credit for anything I do in foreign policy because I didn't go to Harvard."

Lyndon Johnson

"The FBI is filled with Fordham graduates keeping tabs on Harvard men in the State Department."

Daniel Patrick Moynihan

HEALTH WATCH

"The one thing I don't need right now is ulcers."

Arthur Ashe, when asked after his heart surgery if he had any interest in a political career

"My cholesterol's lower than Clinton's, my blood pressure's lower than Clinton's, my weight is less than Clinton's. I am not going to make health an issue."

Bob Dole, running for president at age 72 against Clinton

"It is too bad that this one time while I have something to give everybody—no one comes near me."

Abraham Lincoln, on contracting smallpox

HEROES

"It was involuntary. They sank my ship."

John F. Kennedy, on becoming a hero after his ship sank during World War II

"We can't all be heroes because somebody has to sit on the curb and clap as they go by."

Will Rogers

"Putting and fishing are two of the things I hate the most."

> *George Bush, on the frustrations of golf and fishing*

"Holding office."

> *Calvin Coolidge, when asked if he had any hobbies*

"There are only two occasions when American people respect privacy, especially in presidents. Those are prayer and fishing."

> *Herbert Hoover*

HOCKEY

"All of us in Washington can appreciate what goalies do—we have so many shots taken at us. I wish that as well as a gift jersey, you'd lend me a face mask for the next year or so."

> *Bill Clinton, after the New York*
> *Rangers presented him with a jersey*
> *following their Stanley Cup win*

"I understand the Washington Capitals are going to trade for Wayne Gretzky. What do you think it would take to get him—two first-round draft picks and the state of Texas?"

> *Ronald Reagan*

HONEYMOON

"What honeymoon? If this is the honeymoon, I want a divorce."

> *Carol Mosley-Braun, after being*
> *attacked as soon as she got elected to*
> *the Senate*

J. EDGAR HOOVER

"I'd much rather have that fellow inside my tent pissing out, than outside my tent pissing in."
Lyndon Johnson, on J. Edgar Hoover

HORSE SENSE

"Great American sport. Horseshoes is a very great game. I love it."
Dan Quayle

"There is nothing better for the inside of a man than the outside of a horse."
Ronald Reagan

HOUSE OF
REPRESENTATIVES

"The House looks like more fun. It's like the
Donahue Show. The Senate is like one of those
Sunday-morning public service programs."

> *Phil Donahue, on a possible political
> run*

"He is a man of splendid abilities but utterly
corrupt. Like a rotten mackerel by moonlight, he
shines and stinks."

> *John Randolph, on Edward
> Livingstone, a member of the House
> in the late eighteenth century*

"The right of the minority is to draw its salaries,
and its function is to make a quorum."

> *Thomas Reed, Speaker of the House,
> on the role of the minority party in
> the House*

HUBERT HUMPHREY

"Hubert Humphrey talks so fast that listening to him is like trying to read *Playboy* magazine with your wife turning over the pages."
Barry Goldwater

HURRAY FOR HOLLYWOOD

"Politicians are actors of the first order."
Marlon Brando

"Ronald Reagan just signed the new tax law. But I think he was in Hollywood too long. He signed it, 'Best wishes, Ronald Reagan.'"
Johnny Carson

"You may not know my work, but I've seen all your movies."

Mikhail Gorbachev, upon meeting Paul Newman

"I'm a slime bucket in it, but at least it's not a big part."

> *Henry Kissinger, on how he is*
> *portrayed in the movie* Nixon

"I must say acting was good training for the political life which lay ahead for us."
> *Nancy Reagan*

"Politics is just like show business: you have a hell of an opening, coast for a while, and then have a hell of a close."
> *Ronald Reagan*

"After spending a year in Washington, I long for the realism and sensitivity of Hollywood."
> *Fred Thompson, senator from*
> *Tennessee and former actor*

"No, no—Jimmy Stewart for governor, Ronald Reagan for his best friend."
> *Jack Warner, legendary studio*
> *executive, on Ronald Reagan getting*
> *elected governor of California*

ILLINOIS

"Float like a butterfly, sting like a bee. If you ain't for big Jim, you'll reckon with me."

> *Muhammad Ali, hitting the campaign trail for Illinois governor Jim Thompson*

"To be perfectly blunt, I'm much more intelligent. I'm sorry, but it's true."

> *Dawn Clarke Netsch, telling people why they should vote for her for governor of Illinois and not Jim Edgar*

INAUGURATION

"I feel like the fellow in jail who is watching his scaffold being built."

> *Dwight Eisenhower, watching the construction of stands for the Kennedy inauguration*

INCUMBENTS

"It was easier during the Brezhnev era to get yourself elected to the Supreme Soviet than it is to beat a breathing member of Congress."

> *Lionel Kurst, after losing a congressional race to an incumbent in Kansas*

INDEPENDENTS

"An independent is a person who wants to take the politics out of politics."

> *Adlai Stevenson*

INTELLIGENCE

"An intellectual is a man who takes more words than necessary to tell more than he knows."

> *Dwight Eisenhower*

"If I tell 'em all we both know, it won't take me any longer."

> *Al Smith, after a heckler jeered that*
> *for Smith to tell people all he knew*
> *wouldn't take long*

INVESTIGATIONS

"I not only have no skeletons—I have no closet."
> *Oliver North, when asked if there*
> *were any skeletons in his closet*

"Government investigations have always contributed more to our amusement than they have to our knowledge."
> *Will Rogers*

IRAN

"You need to dance, but dance slowly."
> *Samuel Berger, presidential adviser,*
> *on improving relations with Iran*

ISRAEL

"In Israel, in order to be a realist you must believe in miracles."

David Ben-Gurion

"I ask you to bring greetings from the people of New York to the people of Israel. Our feelings for them run deep, but not so deep that we don't want you to bring home the bacon."

> *John Lindsay, former New York City mayor, to athletes from New York going to Israel to participate in the Maccabiah games*

JAPAN

"When Washington is awake, I am asleep. And even better, when I am awake, Washington is sleeping."

> *Walter Mondale, on being ambassador to Japan*

"Except for his tendency to get angry, arrogant, and sulky, he is the most qualified."

Noboru Takeshita, former Japanese prime minister, on Ryutaro Hashimoto, the Japanese trade minister, running for prime minister

JOBS PROGRAM

"Every once in a while we miss a nuisance, and then find out he's got a political job."

Kin Hubbard

LYNDON JOHNSON

"Son, they are all my helicopters."

Lyndon Johnson, after an officer pointed to a helicopter and said to him, "Your helicopter is over there"

"Hyperbole was to Lyndon Johnson what oxygen is to life."

Bill Moyers

"There is a new fashion sweeping the country: skirts are shorter, pants are tighter, and the LBJ coattails are going out of style."

> *Richard Nixon, on Democratic congressional candidates' reluctance to run in 1966 on President Johnson's coattails*

JACK KEMP

"You could stand up there and strip naked and you're not going to get him to stop talking."

> *Anonymous Secret Service agent, on Kemp*

"John certainly is one of the finest quarterbacks since Jack Kemp."

> *Newt Gingrich, on John Elway*

KENNEDY FAMILY

"The thing you must remember when you play tennis with the Kennedys is that they hate to lose. The safest thing to do if you want to have dinner is to play well but lose."

Art Buchwald

EDWARD KENNEDY

"I admire Ted Kennedy. How many 59-year-olds do you know who still go to Florida for spring break?"

Patrick Buchanan

JOHN F. KENNEDY

"John Fitzgerald Kennedy is sort of an Indian snake charmer."

Dean Acheson

"I would not be truthful if I said I was fully qualified for the office. I do not play the piano, I seldom play golf, and I never play touch football."

>*Barry Goldwater, said during the Kennedy presidency*

"I passed my time reading a book. It was called *JFK: The Man and the Airport.*"

>*Joe Magrane, former baseball player*

HENRY KISSINGER

"Henry Kissinger couldn't see himself running for office and visiting Coney Island eating pizza and blintzes. I sure as hell couldn't see him doing that."

>*George Clark, chair of the New York Republican party, on Kissinger possibly running for governor of New York*

"Joy."

> *Barbara Bush, catching herself before saying what she thought Mayor Koch was full of*

LEADERSHIP

"You do not lead by hitting people over the head. That's assault, not leadership."
> *Dwight Eisenhower*

"Any jackass can kick a barn down, but it takes a carpenter to build it."
> *Sam Rayburn*

"Consensus is the negation of leadership."
> *Margaret Thatcher*

LEGAL AID

"A judge is just a lawyer who somebody's blessed."
William Bennett

"Sometimes I think we're the only two lawyers in Washington who trust each other."
> *Bob Dole, on himself and his wife*
> *Elizabeth*

"He can compress the most words into the smallest ideas better than any man I ever met."
> *Abraham Lincoln, on a lawyer*

LEGISLATION

"Let the other fellows get the headlines. I'll take the laws."
> *Sam Rayburn*

LEGISLATIVE SESSION

"No man's life, liberty, or property are safe while the legislature is in session."

Gideon Tucker, New York judge

"You can lead the House to order, but you can't make it think."

William Weld, former Massachusetts governor, on his relationship with the legislature

LIBERALS

"Liberals think that goats are just sheep from broken homes."

Malcolm Bradbury, British writer

"A liberal is a man who leaves the room when the fight starts."

Heywood Broun

"The liberals can understand everything but people who don't understand them."
Lenny Bruce

"A liberal is a man too broad-minded to take his own side in a quarrel."
Robert Frost

"A liberal is a man who is willing to spend somebody else's money."
Carter Glass

"When you are young and not as experienced, you are more liberal."
Ed Koch

"So much of left-wing thought is a kind of playing with fire by people who don't even know that fire is hot."
George Orwell

"A liberal is a person whose interests aren't at stake at the moment."
Willis Player

"It isn't that liberals are ignorant. It's just that they know so much that isn't so."

Ronald Reagan

"I can remember way back when a liberal was one who was generous with his own money."

Will Rogers

"New York is so full of liberals that you can get an argument if you assert that there are two sexes."

Mort Sahl

ABRAHAM LINCOLN

"He knew the American people better than they knew themselves, and his truth was based upon this knowledge."

Frederick Douglass, on Lincoln

LOBBYISTS

"I can't think of a better way to spend a morning with somebody than riding around a golf course, letting 'em win."

> *Steve Eure, lobbyist, on playing golf with politicians*

"I just want to lobby for God."

> *Billy Graham, on establishing his headquarters in Washington*

"I taught him to be superficial."

> *Steve Martindale, lobbyist, on working with actor Dennis Quaid, who was portraying a lobbyist in a movie*

"A lobbyist is anyone who opposes legislation I want. A patriot is anyone who supports me."

> *James Reed, senator from Missouri*

"A lobbyist is a person that is supposed to help a politician to make up his mind—not only help him but pay him."

> *Will Rogers*

LOSING

"He's gonna win the election with no problem, just like I'm gonna win my next fight."

> *Muhammad Ali, comparing Jimmy Carter's losing the 1980 election and Ali's losing a fight to Larry Holmes*

"If it is a blessing, it is certainly very well disguised."

> *Winston Churchill, told that losing an election was a blessing in disguise*

"I also voted for McGovern and Mondale."

> *Billy Crystal, on predicting Michael Spinks would beat Mike Tyson, a fight Tyson won by knockout in the first minute*

"There are times in politics when you must be on the right side and lose."

> *John Kenneth Galbraith*

"Nothing is so abject and so pathetic as a politician who has lost his job, save only a retired stud horse."

H. L. Mencken

"Finishing second in the Olympics gets you silver. Finishing second in politics gets you oblivion."

Richard Nixon

LOYAL OPPOSITION

"I respect only those who resist me, but I cannot tolerate them."

Charles de Gaulle

"One-fifth of the people are against everything all the time."

Robert Kennedy

"I have spent many years of my life in opposition, and I rather like the role."

Eleanor Roosevelt

MAJORITY LEADER

"One of the baseball team owners approached me and said, 'If you become baseball commissioner, you're going to have to deal with 28 big egos,' and I said for me that's a 72 percent reduction."
George Mitchell, former Senate majority leader

MAJORITY RULES

"In matters of conscience, the law of majority has no place."
Mohandas Gandhi

"Whenever you find that you are on the side of the majority, it is time to reform."
Mark Twain

MALAPROPS AND
FRACTURED SYNTAX

"The undecideds could vote one way or the other."
George Bush

"To higher and higher platitudes."
Richard J. Daley, on the future

"If Lincoln were alive today, he'd be turning over in his grave."
Gerald Ford

"I always watch the Detroit Tigers on radio when I can."
Gerald Ford

"The only way we'll ever get a volunteer army is to draft 'em."
F. Edward Hebert, congressman

"Even Napoleon had his Watergate."
Danny Ozark, baseball manager

"Bobby Knight told me, 'There is nothing that a good defense cannot beat a better offense.' In other words, a good offense wins."

Dan Quayle

"If we do not succeed, then we run the risk of failure."

Dan Quayle

"Sure we've made mistakes, but let's not throw the baby out with the dishes."

Ronald Reagan

"There are four departments. There's the executive, and the legislative, and the judicial—and the Bill of Rights."

Kenneth Wherry, former state senator from Nebraska

"The distinguished senator from Holland."

Kenneth Wherry, introducing Senator Spessard Holland, of Florida

"I have thought for a long time that what the country needs is a president from Massachusetts."
> *Ted Kennedy, endorsing Michael Dukakis for president*

"I'd rather be in jail in Sacramento than the mayor of Boston."
> *Bill Russell*

MAYOR

"I've never been qualified for anything I've done."
> *Sonny Bono, asked if he was qualified to run for mayor of Palm Springs*

"Those teams in the Pacific Coast League were getting a little old. A couple of them wanted me to run for mayor."
> *Dewayne Buice, baseball player, on his long tenure in the minor leagues*

"When all the burdens of the presidency seem unusually heavy, I always remind myself it could be worse—I could be a mayor."

Lyndon Johnson

"Being called untrustworthy by Bud Adams is like being called ugly by a bullfrog."

Bob Lanier, Houston mayor, on a public clash with Bud Adams, owner of the former Houston Oilers

"He should run for president, because if he runs for mayor, he'll beat me."

Jim McConn, another Houston mayor, on the popularity of the Oilers' Earl Campbell

"I didn't think he has to learn anything. . . . I mean, an actor was president of the United States."

Ion Tiriac, asked if former tennis player Ilie Nastase was qualified to run for mayor of Bucharest

WILLIAM McKINLEY

"A man with no more backbone than a chocolate eclair."

> *Theodore Roosevelt, on President McKinley*

MEDIA WATCH

"The 4-H club—hopeless, hysterical, hypochondriacs of history."

> *Spiro Agnew, on the media*

"They're not my type. I like to be around low-class people like reporters."

> *Charles Barkley, on why he did not attend the Clinton inauguration*

"Wooing the press is an exercise roughly akin to picnicking with a tiger. You might enjoy the meal, but the tiger always eats last."

> *Maureen Dowd, New York Times columnist*

"I don't attempt to be a poker player before this crowd."

> *Dwight Eisenhower, at a press conference*

"We are the meanest, nastiest bunch of jealous, petty people who ever lived. You think I wouldn't sell my mother for My Lai?"

> *Seymour Hersh, on investigative reporters*

"The man who reads nothing at all is better educated than the man who reads nothing but newspapers."

> *Thomas Jefferson*

"The fact that a man is a newspaper reporter is evidence of some flaw in character."

> *Lyndon Johnson*

"I am reading it more and enjoying it less."

> *John F. Kennedy, on his press coverage as president*

"The press is like the peculiar uncle you keep in the attic—just one of those unfortunate things."
G. Gordon Liddy

"People everywhere confuse what they read in newspapers with news."
A. J. Liebling

"Reporters are like blackbirds sitting on a telephone wire. One flies off and they all fly off. One flies back and they all fly back."
Eugene McCarthy

"There are honest journalists like there are honest politicians. When bought, they stay bought."
Bill Moyers

"Nobody believes the official spokesman, but everybody trusts an unidentified source."
Ron Nessen

"For the press, progress is not news—trouble is news."
Richard Nixon

"We live under a government of men and morning newspapers."

Wendell Phillips

"My doctors told me this morning my blood pressure is down so low that I can start reading the newspapers."

Ronald Reagan, on recovering from prostate surgery

"The only people who say worse things about politics than reporters do are other politicians."

Andy Rooney

"When a reporter sits down at the typewriter, he's nobody's friend."

Teddy White

MEETINGS

"Meetings are indispensable when you don't want to do anything."

John Kenneth Galbraith

"Say as little as possible while appearing to be awake."

> *William Rogers, former secretary of state, on committee meetings*

MEMOS

"A memorandum is written not to inform the reader but to protect the writer."
> *Dean Acheson*

MIDDLE OF THE ROAD

"The middle of the road is all the usable surface. The extreme right and left are in the gutters."
> *Dwight Eisenhower*

"The middle of the road is where the white line is—that's the worst place to drive."
> *Robert Frost*

"Most political accidents happen in the middle of the road."

Eugene McCarthy

"He who walks in the middle of the road gets hit from both sides."

George Shultz

MISTER POTATO HEAD

"Because there's no golf club called a potato wedge."

Larry Harrington, Democratic consultant, on why Dan Quayle misspelled potato

"You're right phonetically, but what else? . . ."

Dan Quayle, telling a boy at a spelling bee that the boy misspelled potato *because it had an* e *at the end*

"I wouldn't bet the farm on it, but I'd bet the main house. I wouldn't even bet the outhouse on Mondale."

Richard Nixon, on Mondale's chances against Reagan in 1984

MONEY TALKS

"My family got all over me because they said Bush is only for the rich people. Then I reminded them, 'Hey, I'm rich.'"

Charles Barkley, on why he voted for George Bush in 1988

"Washington is a pool of money surrounded by people who want some."

David Brinkley

"In peace and war, it's always money."

David Brinkley

"Have you ever seen a candidate talking to a rich person on television?"

Art Buchwald

"You spend a billion here and a billion there. Sooner or later, it adds up to real money."

Everett Dirksen, Illinois senator

"Money is like an arm or a leg: use it or lose it."

Henry Ford

"There are two things that are important in politics. The first is money, and I can't remember what the second one is."

Mark Hanna

"It's a terribly hard job to spend a billion dollars and get your money's worth."

George Humphrey, former secretary of the Treasury

"I think next time I'll give $600,000."

Roger Tamraz, millionaire oilman, asked in 1998 if his $300,000 gave him access to the White House

"Money is the mother's milk of politics."
Jesse Unruh

MOTHER KNOWS BEST

"Do not run a campaign that would embarrass your mother."

Robert Byrd, advising Democratic presidential candidates in the '84 election

"Mothers all want their sons to grow up to be president, but they didn't want them to become politicians in the process."
John F. Kennedy

MUSICAL INTERLUDE

"I only know two tunes. One of them is 'Yankee Doodle Dandy.' The other isn't."
Ulysses Grant

"The Army played loud music until he gave himself up. If he's convicted, there's talk of sentencing him to the Grammy Awards."

> Bob Hope, on how Manuel Noriega
> was forced out of power in Panama

NAFTA

"I have courted some of these congressmen longer than I courted my wife."

> Lloyd Bentsen, Treasury secretary
> under Bill Clinton, on the NAFTA
> Agreement

"You look at any picture of a politician with some girls and him and at least three of them will be mine. . . . If I really came out and talked, I could have stopped NAFTA."

> Heidi Fleiss, Hollywood madam

"No doughnuts for them."

> Dee Dee Myers, on members of
> Congress who opposed NAFTA
> attending a breakfast celebrating the
> bill signing

"You know, Coach, back in Arkansas where I come from, we have lots of people named Billy Joe. But all of them have last names."

> *Bill Clinton, after being introduced to Billy Joe, football coach at Central State*

"If there's one thing I can't stand, it's a fellow running on his family name."

> *Robert Kennedy, said jokingly about Adlai Stevenson III*

"They don't realize it's not funny after 13,000 times."

> *Tom Sawyer, Ohio congressman, on being asked where Huck Finn was*

"I don't know if it has an *e*."

> *Pete Stark, California congressman, on being asked to spell the name of his young fiancée, Deborah Ann Roderick*

NEGOTIATION

"Compromise used to mean that half a loaf was better than no bread. Among modern statesmen it really seemed to mean that half a loaf is better than a whole loaf."

G. K. Chesterton

"An appeaser is one who feeds a crocodile, hoping it will eat him last."

Winston Churchill

"When you accept our views we shall be in full agreement with you."

Moshe Dayan, said to Cyrus Vance
during a negotiation with Israel

"No nation has friends—only interests."

Charles de Gaulle

"You can't shake hands with a clenched fist."

Indira Gandhi

"Conferences at the top level are always courteous. Name-calling is left to the foreign ministers."
Averell Harriman

"Let us never negotiate out of fear, but let us never fear to negotiate."
John F. Kennedy

"Like dealing with Dad—all give and no take."
John F. Kennedy, on negotiating with Nikita Khrushchev

"The lion and the lamb can lie down together—but the lamb won't get much sleep."
Morris Udall, on negotiations

NEW HAMPSHIRE

"You know, Thomas Wolfe lied, you can come home again. In fact, in my case, the people in New Hampshire insisted on it."
Fritz Hollings, on his short-lived 1984 presidential run

"New Hampshire is all retail politics. Make sure you shake every voter's hand twice."

John Sununu, advice to his son about
New Hampshire politics

NEW YORK

"New York will be happy to share the Giants with our great sister state. Let them be the New York Giants when they win and the New Jersey Giants when they lose."

Mario Cuomo, on the NFL Giants
moving to New Jersey

"If my ancestors had known that Ellis Island was in New Jersey, they might have stayed in Italy."

Rudy Giuliani

"I'm not the type to get ulcers. I give them."

Ed Koch

"The mayor of New York is not a coward . . . and the mayor of New York is also not a schmuck."

Ed Koch, on his refusing to appear
with a Bengal tiger

"I didn't bet him anything. New York doesn't have anything I want."

> *Ann Richards, after the Dallas Cowboys beat the Buffalo Bills in the Super Bowl and Governor Cuomo of New York sent her yellow roses*

RICHARD NIXON

"Other administrations had a love-hate relationship with the press. The Nixon administration had a hate-hate relationship with the press."
John Chancellor

"President Nixon's motto was 'If two wrongs don't make a right, try three.'"
Norman Cousins

"I remember he was so wild that when the word got out he was taking a lesson, the parking lot was emptied of Cadillacs in five minutes. He got better."

> *Max Elbin, pro at a country club where President Nixon played*

"When I first began this campaign, I just wanted to beat Nixon. Now I want to save the country from him."

John F. Kennedy

"He bleeds people. He draws every drop of blood and then drops them from a cliff. He'll blame any person he can put his foot on."

Martha Mitchell

"This administration is not sympathetic to corporations; it is indentured to corporations."

Ralph Nader, on the Nixon presidency

NOMINATIONS

"Senator George McGovern was nominated by the cast of *Hair*."

Tip O'Neill, on the 1972 Democratic presidential nomination

NORTH CAROLINA

"I think it proves that North Carolina doesn't want a senator who knows how to cuss."

Bo Thomas, on losing the North Carolina Democratic senate primary

NUMBERS GAME

"I think Mr. Darman has proved himself an expert on math not adding up."

Bill Clinton, on Richard Darman, George Bush's budget director, adding $60 million to the budget deficit

ORATORY

"I hate to criticize another president, but if anybody knows of another opportunity for a $2 million fee, I wish they'd let me know."

Jimmy Carter, on Ronald Reagan receiving $2 million for a speech in Japan

"Since a politician never believes what he says, he is surprised when others believe him."

Charles de Gaulle

"I never deny, I never contradict; I sometimes forget."

Benjamin Disraeli, on his relationship with Queen Victoria

"I feel like Zsa Zsa Gabor's fifth husband. I know what I'm supposed to do, but I don't know if I can make it interesting."

Al Gore, on being one of the last speakers at a dinner that featured a great many others

"A politician is one who talks himself red, white, and blue in the face."

Clare Boothe Luce

"I have this unfortunate faculty, perhaps, of making the most exciting subject gray."

Claiborne Pell

"Our public men are speaking every day on something—but they ain't saying anything."
Will Rogers

"The most successful politician is he who says what everybody is thinking most often and in the loudest voice."
Theodore Roosevelt

"Man does not live by words alone, despite the fact that sometimes he has to eat them."
Adlai Stevenson

PARDONS

"I asked him for a pardon."
John Tonelli, hockey player, on meeting President Reagan soon after Tonelli was arrested for drunk driving

"There but for the grace of God goes God."
> *Winston Churchill, on the arrogance*
> *of Labour politician Sir Stafford*
> *Cripps*

"If a traveler were informed that such a man was a leader of the House of Commons, he may begin to comprehend how the Egyptians worshiped an insect."
> *Benjamin Disraeli, on Lord John*
> *Russell*

"As usual, the liberals offer a mixture of sound and original ideas. Unfortunately, none of the sound ideas is original and none of the original ideas is sound."
> *Harold Macmillan*

"I will take the examination to test for brain damage if you will."
> *Archie Moore, boxer, to a member of*
> *Parliament who urged that all boxers*
> *be given a test for brain damage*

"He serves his party best who serves his country best."

Rutherford B. Hayes

"It doesn't matter whether you're riding an elephant or a donkey if you're going in the wrong direction."

Jesse Jackson

"Only if they're coming to endorse my opponent."

Don Johnson, Democrat from Tennessee, asked if he wanted Bill Clinton to campaign for him

"I've never belonged to any political party for more than fifteen minutes."

Fiorello La Guardia

"There is no Democratic or Republican way of cleaning the streets."

Fiorello La Guardia

"It's like trying to teach a dog to be a vegetarian."
Richard Lamm, Reform party
candidate, on how political parties
can reform themselves

"I relate to both parties. I eat like an elephant and act like a jackass."
Rich Little

"I'm a Dominican."
Jose Rijo, major-league baseball
player, asked if he was a Democrat
or a Republican

"There's no way in the world you're going to make a political party respectable unless you keep it out of office."
Will Rogers

"All you would have to do to make some men atheists is just to tell them the Lord belonged to the opposition party. After that they could never see any good in him."
Will Rogers

"The more you read and observe about this politics thing, you got to admit that each party is worse than the other."
Will Rogers

"The one that's out always looks the best."
Will Rogers, on political parties

"Liberals feel unworthy of their possessions. Conservatives feel they deserve everything they've stolen."
Mort Sahl

"I don't know a lot about politics, but I know a good party man when I see one."
Mae West

PATRIOTISM

"A politician will do everything to keep his job— even become a patriot."
William Randolph Hearst

"It seems like the less a statesman amounts to, the more he loves the flag."

Kin Hubbard

"Patriotism is the last refuge of a scoundrel."

Samuel Johnson

"Whenever you hear a man speak of his love for his country, it is a sign that he expects to be paid for it."

H. L. Mencken

"In the United States doing good has come to be like patriotism, a favorite device of people with something to sell."

H. L. Mencken

"Men who have offered their lives for their country know that patriotism is not the fear of something, it is the love of something."

Adlai Stevenson

"The rumor is, to boost his approval rating, he may announce he's a lesbian."

Jay Leno, on the floundering
presidential campaign of Ross Perot

PESSIMISM AND OPTIMISM

"The American by nature is an optimist. He is an experimenter, an inventor, and a builder who builds best when called upon to build greatly."

John F. Kennedy

"You've got to be an optimist to be a Democrat, and you've got to be a humorist to stay one."

Will Rogers

"The nice part about being a pessimist is that you are constantly being either proven right or pleasantly surprised."

George Will

"I'm an optimist, but I'm an optimist who carries a raincoat."

Harold Wilson

PHILOSOPHY

"Every man has a right to be wrong in his opinion. But no man has a right to be wrong in the facts."

Bernard Baruch

"I hold it to be the inalienable right of anybody to go to hell in his own way."

Robert Frost

"Extremism in the defense of liberty is no vice. Moderation in the pursuit of justice is no virtue."

Barry Goldwater

"In matters of style, swim with the current. In matters of principle, stand like a rock."

Thomas Jefferson

"Men who are orthodox when they are young are in danger of being middle-aged all their lives."
Walter Lippmann

"I'm a sweet grandmother capable of impaling."
Carrie Meck, first-time congresswoman at age 66, on her philosophy

"There is no record in human history of a happy philosopher."
H. L. Mencken

"Television is to news what bumper stickers are to philosophy."
Richard Nixon

"You can't teach an old dogma new tricks."
Dorothy Parker

"My definition of a free society is a society in which it is safe to be unpopular."
Adlai Stevenson

"The radical of one century is the conservative of
the next."

Mark Twain

POETRY IN MOTION

"You campaign in poetry. You govern in prose."

Mario Cuomo

"When power leads a man toward arrogance,
poetry reminds him of his limitations."

John F. Kennedy

POLITICAL WISDOM

"Knowledge of human nature is the beginning and
end of political education."

Henry Adams

"Practical politics consists in ignoring facts."

Henry Adams

"A real politician has to know the right moment to hit an opponent just a bit below the belt."

Konrad Adenauer

"The standard of intellect in politics is so low that men of moderate mental capacity have to stoop in order to reach it."

Hillaire Belloc

"Too bad that all the people who know how to run the country are busy driving taxicabs and cutting hair."

George Burns

"Sometimes in politics one must deal with skunks, but no one should be fool enough to allow the skunks to choose the weapons."

Joe Cannon

"Politicians are like ships: noisiest when lost in a fog."

Bennett Cerf

"In war, you can only be killed once, but in politics, many times."

Winston Churchill

"In politics what begins in fear usually ends in folly."

Samuel Taylor Coleridge

"The chief idea of the American people is idealism."

Calvin Coolidge

"Politics are too serious a matter to be left to politicians."

Charles de Gaulle

"There is no gambling like politics."

Benjamin Disraeli

"In politics, nothing is contemptible."

Benjamin Disraeli

"How much easier it is to be critical than to be correct."

Benjamin Disraeli

"Politics is far more complicated than physics."

Albert Einstein

"Equations are more important to me, because politics is for the present, but an equation is something for eternity."
Albert Einstein

"In politics and in trade, bruisers and pirates are of better promise than talkers and clerks."
Ralph Waldo Emerson

"Nothing is so admirable in politics as a short memory."
John Kenneth Galbraith

"Take time to deliberate, but when the time for action arrives, stop thought and go in."
Andrew Jackson

"I seldom think of politics more than 18 hours a day."
Lyndon Johnson

"If you're in politics and you can't tell when you walk into a room who's for you and who's against you, then you're in the wrong line of work."
Lyndon Johnson

"Politicians are the same all over: they promise to build a bridge even when there is no river."
Nikita Khrushchev

"Ninety percent of the politicians give the other 10 percent a bad name."
Henry Kissinger

"He'll double-cross that bridge when he comes to it."
Oscar Levant

"I love politics better than buttermilk."
Earl Long

"Politics is the art of looking for trouble, finding it everywhere, diagnosing it incorrectly, and applying the wrong remedies."
Groucho Marx

"The kind of man who wants the government to adopt and enforce his ideas is always the kind of man whose ideas are idiotic."
H. L. Mencken

"In politics stupidity is not a handicap."
Napoleon

"Politicians are interested in the people. Not that this is always a virtue. Dogs are interested in fleas."
P. J. O'Rourke

"Ten percent gall and 90 percent wind."
Boies Penrose, Pennsylvania senator, on politics

"Politicians are people who, when they see the light at the end of the tunnel, go out and buy some more tunnel."
John Quinton

"Politics is the lifeblood of democracy. To call politics dirty is to call democracy dirty."
Nelson Rockefeller

"There is no more independence in politics than there is in jail."
Will Rogers

"Politics ain't worrying this country one-tenth as much as where to find a parking space."
Will Rogers

"I don't make jokes—I just watch the government and report the facts."
Will Rogers

"He knows nothing, he thinks he knows everything—that clearly points to a political career."
George Bernard Shaw

"A government which robs Peter to pay Paul can always depend on the support of Paul."
George Bernard Shaw

"The best politics is good government."
Adlai Stevenson

"Politics is perhaps the only profession for which no preparation is thought necessary."
Robert Louis Stevenson

"Ignorance, idleness, and vice may be sometimes the only ingredients for qualifying as a legislator."
Jonathan Swift

"The ability to change one's view without losing one's gut is the mark of a great politician."
Morris Udall

"All the politicians have three hats: one they wear; the other they throw into the ring; and the third they talk through."
Jimmy Walker

"I am not a politician, and my other habits are good."
Artemus Ward

"What's real in politics is what the voters decide is real."
Ben Wattenberg

"If politicians and scientists were lazier, how much happier we all should be."
Evelyn Waugh

"Politics, like music and golf, is best learned at an early age."

Lawrence Welk

"Every man who takes office in Washington either grows or swells."

Woodrow Wilson

"All things come to him who waits—provided he knows what he is waiting for."

Woodrow Wilson

POLLS

"A straw poll only shows which way the hot air blows."

O. Henry

"How far would Moses have gone if he had taken a poll in Egypt?"

Harry Truman

POST OFFICE

"You can bet that their float will reach the judge's stand by January 6."

Bob Hope, on the U.S. Post Office having a float in the Rose Bowl Parade on January 1

POVERTY

"You've seen one slum and you've seen them all."

Spiro Agnew

"A decent provision for the poor is the true test of civilization."

Samuel Johnson

"The war on poverty has been first in promises, first in politics, first in press releases, and last in performance."

Richard Nixon

"You know you're out of power when your limousine is yellow and your driver speaks Farsi."
James Baker, former top aide to President Bush

"The more you are talked about, the less powerful you are."
Benjamin Disraeli

"Presidents deal with power. Power is real. Power is not pretty."
Lyndon Johnson

"Power is the ultimate aphrodisiac."
Henry Kissinger

"Nearly all men can stand adversity, but if you want to test a man's character, give him power."
Abraham Lincoln

"Power? It's like dead sea fruit: when you achieve it, there's nothing there."
Harold Macmillan

"Power corrupts, but lack of power corrupts
absolutely."

Adlai Stevenson

PRESIDENTIAL ADVISERS

"There is a power struggle going on between
President Reagan's advisers. Moe and Curly are
out. Larry is still in."

Johnny Carson

"Being president is like running a cemetery: you've
got a lot of people under you and nobody's
listening."

Bill Clinton

"Every president needs an SOB—and I'm Nixon's."

H. R. Haldeman

"There's some folks standing behind the President
that ought to get around where he can watch 'em."

Kin Hubbard

PRESIDENTIAL CAMPAIGNS

"If those guys were on *The Dating Game*, nobody would get picked."

> *Roger Ailes, on the 1988 Democratic presidential candidates, among whom were Michael Dukakis, Gary Hart, Joseph Biden, and Richard Gephardt*

"Whenever you order a banana split, they never give you the whole banana. If I'm elected, there'll be a whole banana in every split."

> *George Foreman, on running on a split ticket for president*

"When the voters speak, I listen. Especially when the voter is saying someone else's name."

> *Phil Gramm, withdrawing from a presidential race*

"If I am nominated, I will not run. If I am elected, I will not serve. But if you beg me, I just might reconsider."

> *Alexander Haig*

"When you're out of Bud, you're out of beer."

> *Iowa senator Tom Harkin, on ending his '92 presidential campaign because of lack of funds*

"There is only one problem with this year's presidential election—one of the candidates has to win."

> *Alan King, on the '88 Bush-Dukakis presidential race*

"A headless torso that must find a central nervous system."

> *John Lindsay, former New York City mayor, after the Republicans were defeated in 1964*

"For years, I wanted to run for president in the worst possible way—and I'm sure I did."

> *George McGovern*

"Let us see George Bush reelected this November. And then we'll talk about 1994."

> *Dan Quayle, on his future presidential prospects. The next presidential election was in 1996, not '94*

"I was alarmed at my doctor's report. He said I was sound as a dollar."

> *Ronald Reagan, during his run for the presidency*

"They could look much farther and do much worse—and I think they will."

> *Thomas Reed, House Speaker, on Republican presidential prospects*

"President Ronald Reagan won because he ran against Jimmy Carter. If he had run unopposed, he would have lost."

> *Mort Sahl*

"I would have kicked myself in the ass if I hadn't tried."

> *Arlen Specter, on his short-lived presidential run in '96*

"I have tried to talk about the issues in the campaign and this has sometimes been a lonely road, because I never met anybody coming the other way."

> *Adlai Stevenson, on one of his presidential campaigns*

"The Prime Minister has nothing to hide from the President of the United States."

> *Winston Churchill, on stepping out of*
> *a bath in front of Franklin Roosevelt*

"Yes! I've climbed to the top of that greasy pole."

> *Benjamin Disraeli, on becoming*
> *prime minister of Great Britain*

"The Foreign Relations Committee has had the honor of welcoming the distinguished Prime Minister of India."

> *Jesse Helms, referring to Prime*
> *Minister Benazir Bhutto of Pakistan*

"The main essentials of a successful prime minister are sleep and a sense of history."

> *Harold Wilson*

PRINCIPLES

"I live by my principles, and one of my principles is flexibility."

Everett Dirksen

"Damn your principles! Stick to your party."

Benjamin Disraeli

"A people that values its privileges above its principles soon loses both."

Dwight Eisenhower

"What is morally wrong cannot be politically right."

William Gladstone

"Because I live among mortals and not among angels."

Thaddeus Stevens, nineteenth-century Pennsylvania congressman, on accepting a law that was against his principles

"It is a lot easier to fight for principles than to live up to them."

Adlai Stevenson

PROHIBITION

"A prohibitionist is the sort of man one wouldn't care to drink with, even if he drank."

H. L. Mencken

"Some of my friends drink and some of my friends don't drink. And believe me, I'm for my friends."

James Eli Watson, U.S. senator from Indiana, expressing his views on Prohibition

PUBLIC

"When one is in office, one has no idea how damnable things can feel to the ordinary rank and file of the public."

Winston Churchill

"Danny, the cabin boy for the captain of the *Titanic*."

> *Mario Cuomo, during a feud with Dan Quayle*

"I like getting lectures on values and hard work from Dan Quayle, who recently charged the taxpayers $27,000 for a golf weekend."

> *Molly Ivins, on the former vice president*

"Full Dinner Jacket."

> *Jay Leno, speculating on a name for a movie biography of Dan Quayle, who did not serve in Vietnam*

"I love it when I hear the media describe someone 44 years of age as mature and well seasoned."

> *Dan Quayle, on the media's description of Nolan Ryan, who was the same age as Quayle*

"I love California. I grew up in Phoenix."

> *Dan Quayle*

"Space is almost infinite. As a matter of fact, we think it is infinite."

Dan Quayle

RADICAL

"I never dared be a radical when young for fear it would make me conservative when old."

Robert Frost

RAISE A LITTLE HELL

"I expect to fight that proposition until hell freezes over. Then I propose to start fishing on the ice."

Russell Long

"Governor Reagan and I have one thing in common: we both played football. I played for Michigan. He played for Warner Brothers."
Gerald Ford

"Ronald Reagan is not a typical politician because he doesn't know how to lie, cheat, and steal. He's always had an agent do that."
Bob Hope

"People here may be sharply divided over the Reagan administration's policies—but they admire Ronald Reagan for not getting involved in them."
Edward Kennedy

"It's like meeting Santa Claus. You go in, shake his hand, have your picture taken, and then you leave."

Ray Mancini, boxer, on meeting President Reagan

"You've got to be careful quoting Ronald Reagan, because when you quote him accurately it's called mudslinging."

> *Walter Mondale*

"Everyone is wondering why Reagan is in Texas shooting turkeys when he should be in Washington firing them."

> *Robert Neumann, Democratic*
> *National Committee, during one of*
> *President Reagan's vacations in Texas*

"They say hard work never hurt anybody, but I figure why take the chance."

> *Ronald Reagan*

"It was the result of many years spent as a mediocre showbiz figure listening to rich, crotchety Republicans yearning for a return to the good old days."

> *Mike Royko, on Reaganomics*

"His penmanship left a lot to be desired."

> *Joe Sambito, former major league*
> *baseball player, after getting Ronald*
> *Reagan's autograph on a baseball*

"He is attempting a great breakthrough in political technology—he has been perfecting the Teflon-coated presidency."

Patricia Schroeder

"It's my fault. We should have given him better parts."

Jack Warner, on Ronald Reagan becoming governor of California

REFORM

"All reformers, however strict their social conscience, live in houses just as big as they can pay for."

Logan Pearsall Smith

"A reformer is a man who rides through a sewer in a glass-bottom boat."

James Walker

RELIGION

"In a very Christian way, as far as I'm concerned, he can go to hell."

Jimmy Carter, on Jerry Falwell

"God Almighty was satisfied with 10 commandments. Mr. Wilson requires 14 points."

Georges Clemenceau, on Woodrow Wilson's proposed 14 points for creation of the League of Nations

"An atheist is a guy who watches a Notre Dame–SMU football game and doesn't care who wins."

Dwight Eisenhower

"Mother Teresa does not get tickets."

Rudy Giuliani, on Mother Teresa asking the mayor to exempt nuns from getting parking tickets in New York City

"If people want a sense of purpose, they should get it from their archbishops. They should not hope to receive it from their politicians."

Harold Macmillan

"When you said you were going to give up something for Lent, I never thought it would be politics."

Patricia Paxson, mother of Congressman Bill Paxson, in 1998, shortly after his decision to leave the House of Representatives

"Some of us worship in churches, some in synagogues, some on golf courses."

Adlai Stevenson

"I believe if we introduced the Lord's Prayer here, senators would propose a large number of amendments to it."

Henry Wilson, senator from Massachusetts

"It seems to be a law of nature that Republicans are more boring than Democrats."

Stewart Alsop

"Dressing is a matter of taste, and I've met very few Republicans with good taste."

Willie Brown, San Francisco mayor

"I was kind of jealous that the Republicans had appropriated such a nice animal as their symbol. I think they're fascinating."

Bill Clinton, on the elephants he saw while he was on a safari

"Lincoln was right about not fooling all the people all the time. But the Republicans haven't given up trying."

Lyndon Johnson

"I think that it is very important that we have a two-party country. I am a fellow that likes small parties, and the Republican party is about the size I like."

Lyndon Johnson

"The function of liberal Republicans is to shoot the wounded after battle."
Eugene McCarthy

"In this world of sin and sorrow, there is always something to be thankful for. As for me, I realize that I am not a Republican."
H. L. Mencken

"We're the party that wants to see an America in which people can still get rich."
Ronald Reagan

"Republicans believe every day is the Fourth of July, but Democrats believe every day is April 15."
Ronald Reagan

"You can't make the Republican party pure by more contributions, because contributions are what got it where it is today."
Will Rogers

"The dinosaur wing of the party."
Adlai Stevenson, on conservative Republicans

"There are some Republicans I would trust with anything—anything, that is, except public office."
Adlai Stevenson

"The Republican party makes even its young men seem old; the Democratic party makes even its old men seem young."
Adlai Stevenson

"I don't give 'em hell. I just tell the truth and they think it's hell."
Harry Truman, on Republicans

RETIREMENT

"When the curtain falls, the best thing an actor can do is go away."
Harold Macmillan, retiring from Parliament

"Sit on my rear end."
Thurgood Marshall, when asked what he would do upon retiring from the Supreme Court

"Come to think of it, things won't be that different after all."

> *Ronald Reagan, after saying that he would continue to take long naps when his presidency was finished*

"Most of the visitors come here to see if the animal is still alive. But I fool 'em: I stay in my office most of the day."

> *Harry Truman, in 1959, on visitors to the Truman Library*

NELSON ROCKEFELLER

"A lot of people were surprised that Ford picked Nelson Rockefeller to run with him; after all, Rocky had tried to get the job of president three times himself. That's like asking Morris the Cat to watch your tuna salad."

> *Bob Hope*

"In Franklin Roosevelt there died the greatest American friend we have ever known and the greatest champion of freedom who has ever brought help and comfort from the New World to the Old."

Winston Churchill

"Meeting Franklin Roosevelt was like opening the finest bottle of champagne; knowing him was like drinking it."

Winston Churchill

"A second-class intellect—but a first-class temperament."

Oliver Wendell Holmes, on FDR

"He would rather follow public opinion than lead it."

Harry Hopkins

THEODORE ROOSEVELT

"That damned cowboy is president of the United States."

> *Mark Hanna*

"My father always wanted to be the corpse at every funeral, the bride at every wedding, and the baby at every christening."

> *Alice Roosevelt Longworth, on her father, Teddy*

"Do not hit at all if it can be avoided, but never hit softly."

> *Theodore Roosevelt*

SCANDALS

"It is very disappointing and hurtful. How come nobody ever thought that I had an affair with anyone?"

> *Barbara Bush, referring to the sex scandals involving President Clinton*

"I won't say he flew a lot. But he won't start a cabinet meeting until the seat backs and tray tables are locked into the upright position."

> *Bob Dole, on the scandal involving John Sununu and the use of planes for personal matters*

"He asked if it was, in fact, an April Fool's joke."

> *Mike McCurry, on President Clinton's reaction to the Paula Jones lawsuit being dropped on April 1*

"I want a blood test."

> *Donald Regan, on his being linked, while secretary of the Treasury, to the savings-and-loan scandal*

SECOND TERM

"It's golf, golf, golf—interspersed with politics."

> *John Breaux, Louisiana senator, on the interests of Bill Clinton in his second term*

"Anyone can be elected once by accident, but with the second term, it's worth paying attention."
Sam Rayburn

SENATE

"No man, however strong, can serve ten years as schoolmaster, priest, or senator and remain fit for anything else."
Henry Adams

"Senate: a body of elderly gentlemen charged with high duties and misdemeanors."
Ambrose Bierce

"No, but it can be rented."
John Breaux, Louisiana senator,
asked if his vote could be bought

"The boys are in such a mood that if someone introduced the Ten Commandments, they'd cut them down to seven."
Norris Cotton, U.S. senator

"Our intent will not be to create gridlock. Oh, except maybe from time to time."

> Robert Dole, on negotiations with the
> Clinton administration

"Trouble is, there are too many Democratic and Republican senators and not enough United States senators."

> Ed Ford

"Senators are expected to shave and wear socks."

> John Grisham, author, on not
> running for the Senate

"The Senators were never very good, but not much has changed in Washington. The senators they have there still aren't very good."

> Richard Nixon, comparing the former
> Washington Senators baseball team to
> the U.S. Senate

"While this is said to be the most exclusive club in the world, no one ever said it was the most productive."

> David Pryor, Arkansas senator

"The Senate is a nice, quiet sort of place where good representatives go when they die."

Thomas Reed

"We got wind in the Senate where we paid to get wisdom."

Will Rogers

"Our constitution protects aliens, drunks, and U.S. senators."

Will Rogers

"About all I can say for the United States Senate is that it opens with a prayer and ends with an investigation."

Will Rogers

SEX

"My theory is, don't do it before you're 21 and then don't tell me about it."

Hillary Clinton, on sex

"The Gulf War was like teenage sex. We got in too soon and out too soon."

Tom Harkin, Iowa senator

"Dan would rather play golf than have sex any day."

Marilyn Quayle

SHORT PEOPLE

"Secretary Reich could almost live in there."

Bill Clinton, looking at a Lego model of the White House and referring to Secretary of Labor Robert Reich, who is 4 feet 10 inches tall

"I defy anyone to come up with a smaller, more efficient labor secretary. I can get by on 800 calories a day."

Robert Reich, on calls for a smaller federal government

SKIING

"We skiers know that falling down isn't important, it's getting up again."
Gerald Ford

SMOKE IN YOUR EYES

"What this country needs is a really good five-cent cigar."
Thomas Marshall, former vice president

"You better take advantage of the good cigars. You don't get much else on that job."
Tip O'Neill, advice to Walter Mondale on his vice presidency

SOCIALISTS

"All socialists are either dumb or romantic."
William Buckley

"The function of socialism is to raise suffering to a higher level."

Norman Mailer

"Many people consider the things government does for them to be social progress—but they consider the things government does for others as socialism."

Earl Warren

SOVIET UNION

"Russia is a riddle wrapped in a mystery inside an enigma."

Winston Churchill

"You start out giving your hat, then you give your coat, then your shirt, then your skin, and finally your soul."

Charles de Gaulle, on negotiations with the Russians

"The Soviets approach arms control much the same way Andy Warhol approached art: anything you can get away with."

Jack Kemp

SPORTS

"I'd rather be on the sports page than on the front page."

Gerald Ford

"I always turn to the sports section first. The sports section records people's accomplishments; the front page, nothing but men's failures."

Earl Warren

STATESMEN

"The first requirement of a statesman is that he be dull."

Dean Acheson

"The difference between a politician and a statesman is: a politician thinks of the next election and a statesman thinks of the next generation."

> *James Freeman Clarke, Unitarian minister*

"A politician is a person with whose politics you don't agree; if you agree with him, he is a statesman."

> *David Lloyd George*

"You have to get the election certificate before you can be a statesman."

> *Lyndon Johnson*

"At home you always have to be a politician. When you're abroad, you almost feel yourself a statesman."

> *Harold Macmillan*

"The statesman shears the sheep; the politician skins them."

> *Austin O'Malley*

"A statesman is a successful politician who is dead."

> *Thomas Reed*

ADLAI STEVENSON

"Adlai Stevenson has a genius for saying the right thing at the right time—to the wrong people."

> *Joe E. Lewis*

"I feel like Adlai Stevenson, the perennial candidate."

> *Colin McLaughlin, major-league pitcher who has had tryouts with many teams*

"If the electoral college ever gave an honorary degree, it ought to go to Adlai Stevenson."

> *Bill Wirtz*

"I feel like the Susan Lucci of the administration."
> *Bruce Babbitt, on constantly being*
> *mentioned as a Supreme Court*
> *candidate but never being nominated*

"You'll hear from 20 senators before you get to speak. It may be the most painful part of the process."
> *Joseph Biden, during the Clarence*
> *Thomas hearings*

"It gives new meaning to the expression 'High Court.'"
> *James Brady, on Douglas Ginsburg, a*
> *Supreme Court nominee who*
> *admitted to having smoked pot*

"That's kind of ironic, don't you think? Here's a guy who was an All-American football star in college. Then, when he gets a job, he spends 30 years sitting on a bench."
> *Jay Leno, on former football star and*
> *Supreme Court Justice Byron*
> *"Whizzer" White*

"The people can change Congress, but only God can change the Supreme Court."

George Norris

"That was one time when my integrity triumphed over my judgment."

Antonin Scalia, on defeating Senator Howard Metzenbaum in tennis before the Senate confirmed Scalia's appointment to the Supreme Court

WILLIAM HOWARD TAFT

"He looked at me as if I was a side dish he hadn't ordered."

Ring Lardner, on the portly former president

TALK TOO MUCH

"Silence is the best substitute for brains ever invented."

Henry Ashurst, former senator

"My mother said I should never give a talk after seven o'clock at night."

> Bill Clinton, after saying a
> misstatement of his taxes was made
> because of fatigue

"I find it more interesting when I speak than when I listen."

> Barney Frank, on being a fast talker

"It ain't a bad plan to keep still occasionally, even when you know what you're talking about."

> Kin Hubbard

"The most valuable of all talents is that of never using two words when one will do."

> Thomas Jefferson

"People are generally amused that I would take an interest in any forum that would require me to stop talking for three hours."

> Henry Kissinger, on his love of opera

"No one has a finer command of language than the person who keeps his mouth shut."

> Sam Rayburn

"I have sat in the Speaker's chair and watched many a congressman talk himself out of Congress."
Sam Rayburn

"I don't mind how much my ministers talk as long as they do what I say."
Margaret Thatcher

"Swearing is an art form. You can express yourself much more directly, much more exactly, much more succinctly with properly used curse words."
Coleman Young, former Detroit mayor, on his occasional use of profanity

TAXES

"An income-tax form is like a laundry list—either way you lose your shirt."
Fred Allen

"Tax reform is when you take the taxes off things that have been taxed in the past and put taxes on things that haven't been taxed before."
Art Buchwald

"The rich aren't like us; they pay less taxes."
Peter De Vries

"I want to find out who this FICA guy is and how come he's taking so much of my money."
Nick Kypreos, hockey player, on having the opportunity to meet President Clinton when the New York Rangers won the Stanley Cup

"The liberal Democrats want to give us free condoms—and the conservative Republicans want to give us 500 bucks every time they won't work. What a great deal."
Jay Leno, on Bob Dole's proposed tax cut of $500 for each child

"Tax reform means 'don't tax you, don't tax me, tax that fellow behind the tree.'"
Russell Long

"Save our trees. Stop printing tax forms."
Robert Obren

"The distance between the present system and our proposal is like comparing the distance between the Model T and the space shuttle. And I should know—I've seen both."

> *Ronald Reagan, on his tax-reform plan*

"The taxpayer—that's someone who works for the federal government but doesn't have to take a civil service examination."

> *Ronald Reagan*

"When everybody has got money they cut taxes, and when they're broke they raise 'em. That's statesmanship of the highest order."

> *Will Rogers*

"The income tax has made more liars out of the American people than golf has."

> *Will Rogers*

"Even when you make a tax form out on the level, you don't know when it's through if you are a crook or a martyr."

> *Will Rogers*

"There was a time when a fool and his money were soon parted; now it happens to everybody."

Adlai Stevenson, on taxes

"What's the difference between a taxidermist and a tax collector? The taxidermist takes only your skin."

Mark Twain

TENNIS

"They're happy to play with a senator—while I'm happy to play with someone good."

John Breaux, on playing tennis with interns

"Tennis is not a matter of life and death. It's more important than that."

David Dinkins, former New York City mayor

"People trust their tennis partners—even their opponents."

Karen Feld, columnist, on why so many political insiders play tennis

"I needed all the help I can get."

Gerald Ford, on adding a graphite racket to his game

"I used to play when I was younger, but I don't anymore because I can't get the horse on the court."

Ronald Reagan, on why he prefers horseback riding to tennis

TERM LIMITS

"Asking an incumbent member of Congress to vote for term limits is a bit like asking a chicken to vote for Colonel Sanders."

Bob Inglis

"Limit the terms of members of Congress, especially members of the House and members of the Senate."

Dan Quayle

"We do have a little trouble competing with Versailles and places like that."

> *Barbara Bush, on the idea of having a major summit in Houston*

"I'm not going to say too much about it. He might end up being our governor, and I don't want him to raise my taxes."

> *Scott Livingstone, baseball player, on getting a hit off Texan Nolan Ryan*

"You just work like a dog, do well, the test scores are up, the kids are looking better, the dropout rate is down, and all of a sudden you've got some jerk who's running for public office telling everybody it's all a sham and it isn't real."

> *Ann Richards, on her gubernatorial opponent George W. Bush*

"Margaret Thatcher is my candidate."

> *Bowie Kuhn, on whom he would recommend as the next baseball commissioner*

"We're a couple of conservative guys."

> *John McEnroe, on why he thought Margaret Thatcher was such a big fan of his*

"She has Marilyn Monroe's mouth and Caligula's eyes."

> *François Mitterrand, on Thatcher*

"No woman in my time will be prime minister. . . . Anyway, I wouldn't want to be prime minister. You have to give yourself 100 percent."

> *Margaret Thatcher, said in 1969*

TRADING CARDS

"I don't dare ask how many hundreds of George Bush cards you have to trade to get one Michael Jordan."

> *George Bush, on presidential trading cards*

HARRY TRUMAN

"The captain with the mighty heart."
> *Dean Acheson, on Truman*

"Shirt salesman from Kansas City."
> *John Foster Dulles*

"If I'd have known how much packing I'd have to do, I'd have run again."
> *Harry Truman, on leaving the Oval Office after his first full term*

"He loved politicians—even Republicans."
> *Margaret Truman, on her father*

JOHN TYLER

"He has been called a mediocre man; but this is unwarranted flattery. He was a politician of monumental littleness."

Theodore Roosevelt, on John Tyler

UN–AMERICAN ACTIVITIES COMMITTEE

"They'll hang anyone who ever scratched his ass during the national anthem."

Humphrey Bogart, on the House Un-American Activities Committee

"I've said many a time that I think the Un-American Activities Committee in the House of Representatives was the most un-American thing in America."

Harry Truman

UNEMPLOYMENT

"The unemployment numbers are down to the lowest in 25 years. . . . The principal credit goes to Janet Reno, who continues to appoint special prosecutors."

> *Dick Armey, House majority leader,*
> *on Attorney General Reno's*
> *appointment of several special*
> *prosecutors in recent years*

"When a great many people are unable to find work, unemployment results."
> *Calvin Coolidge*

"The Democrats have an answer to the unemployment problem. They're all running for the presidency."

> *Bob Hope, on the many Democrats*
> *running for president in 1988*

UNITED NATIONS

"After four years at the United Nations, I sometimes yearn for the peace and tranquility of a political convention."

> *Adlai Stevenson, on his tenure as the U.S. ambassador to the United Nations*

"There is nothing more horrifying than stupidity in action."

> *Adlai Stevenson, on the U.N.*

"The United Nations is just like football—a series of huddles always followed by outbursts of violence."

> *George Will*

VICE PRESIDENT

"So that the President will be safe from getting shot."

> *Muhammad Ali, on why he would like to be vice president*

"He's a very good player. I think he's a much better player than he is a vice president."

> *Art Buchwald, on George Bush's tennis game*

"Inside work with no heavy lifting."

> *Bob Dole, describing the vice presidency*

"It would be all right with me. I'd probably get a car and driver out of it."

> *Bob Dole, on rumors in 1988 that Elizabeth Dole would become George Bush's vice-presidential candidate*

"A spare tire on the automobile of government."

> *John Nance Garner, vice president under Franklin Roosevelt, on the office*

"That was the ultimate heckle."

> *Al Gore, after someone yelled out, during his run for the presidency in 1988, that he would make a good vice president*

"I have not been calling the signals. I have been in the position of a lineman doing some of the downfield blocking."

> *Hubert Humphrey, on the vice presidency*

"I'm like the girl next door—always available, but you don't necessarily think about marriage."

> *Hubert Humphrey, on making known his availability for the vice presidency*

"Something remarkable. Like him asking."

> *Bob Kerrey, senator from Nebraska, on what it would take for him to be Bill Clinton's vice-presidential candidate*

"One time there were two brothers. One ran away to sea, the other was elected vice president, and nothing was ever heard of either of them again."

> *Thomas Marshall, former vice president*

"In golf, you keep your head down and follow through. In the vice presidency, you keep your head up and follow through. It's a big difference."

> *Dan Quayle*

"There is absolutely no circumstance whatever under which I would accept that spot. Even if they tied and gagged me, I would find a way to signal by wiggling my ears."

> *Ronald Reagan, on possibly being offered the vice presidency in 1968*

"The man with the best job in the country is the vice president. All he has to do is get up every morning and say, 'How's the president?'"

> *Will Rogers*

"The favorite indoor sport around Washington—making fun of vice presidents."

> *Dean Rusk*

"I am against vice in every form, including the vice presidency."

> *Morris Udall, on refusing the opportunity to be Jimmy Carter's running mate*

"I do not propose to be buried until I am really dead."

> *Daniel Webster, rejecting a vice presidential nomination*

"I should say not. The truth alone would beat me . . . not to mention what the opposition would dig up."

> *William Wheeler, vice president*
> *under Rutherford B. Hayes, on*
> *running for president*

"The chief embarrassment in discussing this office is that in explaining how little there is to be said about it, one has evidently said all there is to say."

> *Woodrow Wilson, on the vice*
> *presidency*

VICES

"It has been my experience that folks who have no vices have very few virtues."

> *Abraham Lincoln*

VOMIT

"I just wanted to get a little attention."
> *George Bush, after vomiting on*
> *Japanese prime minister Kiichi*
> *Miyazawa*

"This must be Bush's dog."
> *Bob Kerrey, after a dog threw up on*
> *him right after President Bush threw*
> *up on the Japanese prime minister*

WAR AND PEACE

"War is too important to be left to the generals."
> *Georges Clemenceau*

"I studied dramatics under him for 12 years."
> *Dwight Eisenhower, on General*
> *Douglas MacArthur*

"There never was a good war or a bad peace."
> *Benjamin Franklin*

"Universal peace sounds ridiculous to the head of an average family."
Kin Hubbard

"Military intelligence is a contradiction in terms."
Groucho Marx

"A political war is one in which everyone shoots from the lip."
Raymond Moley

"Peace is not the absence of conflict but the ability to cope with conflict by peaceful means."
Ronald Reagan

"The United States never lost a war or won a conference."
Will Rogers

GEORGE WASHINGTON

"George Washington, as a boy, was ignorant of the commonest accomplishments of youth—he could not even lie."

Mark Twain

WATERGATE

"Once the toothpaste is out of the tube, it's hard to get back in."

H. R. Haldeman, on Watergate

"The illegal we do immediately. The constitutional takes a little longer."

Henry Kissinger, on Watergate

"There will be no whitewash in the White House."

Richard Nixon

"I have many friends who live there, and they tell me it's very nice."

> *Richard Nixon, asked about the*
> *Watergate Hotel, years after resigning*
> *his presidency*

"What was I supposed to say? 'Glad you got over Watergate'?"

> *Steve Sax, former Dodgers second*
> *baseman, after Richard Nixon visited*
> *the team and told Sax he was glad*
> *he was over his throwing problems*

"I'm not going to comment on a third-rate burglary attempt."

> *Ron Ziegler, Nixon administration*
> *press secretary, on Watergate*

WEIGHTY AFFAIRS OF STATE

"He ate everything but the drapes. . . . He's a man who does like to put it down."

> *Tom Brokaw, on Bill Clinton*

"I won my age and body-fat division."
> *Bill Clinton, on running a five-kilometer race*

"The best way to lose weight is to close your mouth—something very difficult for a politician."
> *Ed Koch*

"The Secret Service has signs all over the island saying, 'Please do not feed the President.'"
> *David Letterman, during one of President Clinton's vacations on Martha's Vineyard*

"Thank you for the flowers. They were delicious."
> *George Reedy, overweight press secretary to Presidents Kennedy and Johnson, on being sent flowers at the hospital*

"Not with this president."
> *Donna Shalala, Health and Human Services secretary under Bill Clinton, on the suggestion of a tax on junk food*

"When a man weighs 295 pounds, you have to give him some opportunity to make his legs and muscles move, and golf offers that opportunity."
William Howard Taft

WHITE HOUSE

"Because I found out that they liked the court more than they liked me."
> *Marlin Fitzwater, press secretary to President Bush, on why he stopped inviting dates to play tennis on the White House courts*

"I'm looking forward to your passing the ball around here, but please take it easy. We only rent."
> *Gerald Ford, to the Harlem Globetrotters during one of their visits to the White House*

"Living over the shop."
> *Lady Bird Johnson, on living in the White House*

"This is the first time that sleeping in the wrong bed has actually gotten him out of trouble."

> *Jay Leno, on President Clinton sleeping at Blair House the night a plane crashed at the White House*

"Now I suppose we'll have to have the Trumans over to our house."

> *Oscar Levant, after he and his wife were invited to dinner at the White House*

"This is not my house. It's the people's house."

> *Franklin Pierce*

"If you need a plumber, you can get a plumber."

> *Nancy Reagan, on why it is nice to live in the White House*

"The White House is the leakiest place I've ever been in."

> *Ronald Reagan*

WHITEWATER

"You drag hundred-dollar bills through trailer parks, and there's no telling what you'll find."
James Carville, Clinton adviser, on the Whitewater investigation

"What did the President know, and when did Hillary tell him?"
Al D'Amato

"Nobody's bulletproof in this White House. Every single person here serves at the pleasure of the President. It's a tough neighborhood."
Dee Dee Myers, after the leaking of Whitewater information to the press

WINNING

"Forget that I am president of the United States. I am Warren Harding, playing with some friends, and I'm going to beat the hell out of them."
Warren Harding, on golf

"Winning is like shaving—you do it every day or you wind up looking like a bum."
Jack Kemp

WISCONSIN

"There are those in Wisconsin who say we'd be better off if I missed all those votes."
William Proxmire, on his record of over 10,000 consecutive roll calls in the Senate

WOMEN

"Toughness doesn't have to come in a pin-striped suit."
Diane Feinstein

"In politics, if you want anything said, ask a man; if you want anything done, ask a woman."
Margaret Thatcher

WORDS AND DEEDS

"'No comment' is a splendid expression. I'm using it again and again."
Winston Churchill

"That's a good question. Let me try to evade you."
Paul Tsongas, after being asked a tough question during his presidential run in '92

YOUTH MOVEMENT

"A few months ago Kennedy's mother said, 'You have a choice. Do you want to go to camp this year or run for president?'"
Bob Hope, on JFK running for president at a young age

"Mr. Dewey has tossed his diapers into the ring."
Harold Ickes, on Thomas Dewey running for president at a young age

INDEX

*An asterisk appears before names that
are referred to in a quote. All other
names are the actual sources of a quote.

230

246